IVA

Lost
in the
VALLEY

A True Story of an Addict's Journey To Recovery

Set To Shine Publishing

Published by
Set To Shine Publishing
P.O. Box 564
Powder Springs, GA 30127

Edited by Chaun Archer
Book Cover & Interior Design by Chaun Archer - AVIDMultimedia.net

ISBN-13: 978-0982227237
ISBN-10: 098222723X
Library of Congress Control Number: 2015904205

Printed in the United States of America.

First Edition

10 9 8 7 6 5 4 3 2 1

Dedication

~ For my mother Dilcy Mae Vereen, if it had not been for your love, strength, prayers and patience, I just don't know where I would be. You are forever loved and missed. ~

Table of Contents

Table of Contents iii

Acknowledgements v

Introduction ix

1 A Purpose For Pain 13

2 Innocence Lost 23

3 He Loves Me, He Loves Me Not 30

4 The Beginning of the End 37

5 Decisions 47

6 The Old Manipulator 55

7 What's Done in the Dark 65

8 Addiction 72

9 Always Looking For Love 80

10 Slippery Slope 90

11 Big City Streets 104

12 The Lion and the Prey 112

13 Love, Marriage and Addiction 118

14 Knowledge and Awareness 126

15 Sin Cycles: Wash, Rinse, Repeat 133

16 A Real Change 141

17 Forgiveness and Deliverance: My Path To Recovery 149

18 Encouragement 153

Resources 160

Acknowledgements

I would like to thank God who is the Head of my life for sustaining me and for keeping me until I was able to stand on my own. Without Christ Jesus I'm nothing, thank You dear Lord for saving me!

I must give a special thanks to my Editor, and book designer, Chaun Archer for her hard work, expertise, wisdom, encouragement and insight through this whole process. Thank you so much for helping to put this together. I couldn't have finished this without you. Truly I thank God for you and I look forward to many more projects together!

To my children, Laquan, Devon, Marsell, Baby Boy, Daquan, Kenny and Princess, I want to personally tell you all just how much I love and appreciate each of you. Thank you for your patience with me through it all. I also want to thank you for not judging me for my past mistakes and for encouraging me to get my story out. Forgive me for not being the mother you all needed early on, but I thank God for turning it all around for our good. Today I know I am blessed to have each of you as my children, you all mean the world to me. Just as you have inspired and encouraged me to keep going, I want you all to keep going and growing in the things of God, may He continue to bless you all greatly and abundantly in Jesus Name!

My Mother, Dilcy Mae Vereen, thank you for being the foundation and glue that held our family together; truly you are loved and missed. I thank you for the great job you did with us all, it is my goal to continue to make you proud. The best gift you gave me was the gift of Christ. Today I understand things a lot better. I am now the woman of God that you always believed I could be, saved, sanctified, Holy Ghost-filled and water baptized! Thank you mom, you are the MVP! I love you mommy!

My dearest Liana, I want to tell you just how much I love you. You held me down and didn't judge me regardless of the state of mind I was in. You saw the best in me, and challenged anyone who didn't. Thank you for always being there for me sis, I love you and appreciate you more than words can say. Keep going and growing in the things of God, and allow Him to take you places you've never been before!

To my handsome brother Levance and my beautiful sisters Margaret and Buffy I want to thank you guys for being there for me the best you knew how. Thank you for not judging me, but for supporting me through those hard times, I love you guys dearly!

Chief Apostle, Bishop Marion E. Johnson, my spiritual mother, thank you for your love, wisdom, time and patience with me. It took me traveling miles to meet a woman strong enough to handle and mentor me. I know that God has placed you in my life. I have learned a great deal from you and I thank you for allowing God to use you to get me where I need to be in Him. There was a lot I just didn't understand but you still didn't give up on me, you embraced me and loved me through it all, thank you Apostle, aka Mom, I love you!

Daddy, although we had a rough start, I thank God for bringing both of us out into the light. I understand the past a lot better today. Without you Daddy I wouldn't be here, thank you for not giving up. I didn't realize the pain you were in until I experienced it for myself but it's over now, today we are new and our pasts are over. God bless and keep you daddy. I love you dearly!

Senior Bishop A. Ralph Johnson, my spiritual father, thank you for your love and support as well. Pop-pop, I love you and pray for nothing but the best for you and mom.

My dear sister friend Joanne, thank you for calling me to check on me from time to time. Thank you for being there for me and for your love, support and prayers. May God continue to shine His light on and through you always.

Please forgive me if I missed anyone, I want to thank everyone who helped me along my journey. It has been tough re-visiting certain time periods of my past, but also a healing process. This book had to be written for my growth and now I can move forward because my past is truly behind me. Thank you all from the bottom of my heart!

Introduction

Drug addiction does not have to be a death sentence. For many years I believed I wasn't good enough to be loved. As a result of abuse, I developed low self- esteem and for a long time I avoided facing the truth. I needed help but who was I to go to? I tried N.A. (Narcotics Anonymous) and A.A. (Alcohol Anonymous), rehab after rehab, group after group but still no relief from the bowels of death. The drugs were killing me from the inside out. My mind was a mess and I began to lose all hope.

"Help me, help me!" my soul cried out, but I thought no one heard me. "I'm tired, oh God, what am I going to do now?" I have disappointed everyone who ever loved me. I hurt those who cared for me. I was lost to the streets, in the valley of the shadow of death, where drug addiction was a common way of life. Who do I go to? Who is going to help me? Who will ever love me again? The guilt, shame and fear of people finding out what I had become, kept me running from house to house, person to person, and rock to rock. I was running from myself, I was dying. I thought of God at the time as a being far away, but not someone who could actually really and truly help me. He wasn't real to me yet. I was brought up in churches, our mother made us go, but me living for God was a far out thought from the confused state of mind I was in at that time. It took some time but I found out what it really meant to believe.

I was taught to believe that we overcome by our testimonies, I now have learned that the more you hide things, the more those things will poison you from the inside out. Shame has a way of keeping us in bondage. However, The Bible tells us, "There is therefore now no condemnation to them which are in Christ Jesus." Romans 8:1. In this book I am being completely open and transparent about my time in the pit of despair, because this is how I have gained my deliverance.

Throughout this book you will see references to The Bible, this is because I am a Believer. I believe in God, and I am a Christian. The Bible is the basis of my faith. I use it as a guide, and draw inspiration and strength from the words within. I believe that God created all things, is the source of life, and deeply cares for us. I also believe that no matter where you are or how insignificant or meaningless you believe your life is, you have a purpose to fulfill while on this earth.

Why do bad things happen to us? Where was God when I was going through the most difficult pain or loss in my life? You may ask these questions, and I'm here to tell you, He was there. Our storms are designed to take us to our next level by faith. Some seasons and even storms in our lives may seem impossible to bear, but God will not give us more than we can handle. Whatever we are going through, He has already equipped us to handle it; and when we are weak we can always ask for His help. Sometimes we are too blinded by pride, pain, and circumstances to ask God for His guidance and strength in those moments. There is a growing process that takes place while we are in a struggle big or small. In order to grow, there will be growing pains; but after the pain comes the maturity, and after the maturity comes the change.

Even I have asked these questions on my journey. There were times that were the lowest, darkest moments in my life and I looked around and felt as if I was alone. Times when I hadn't bathed in a while, and I was wearing the same clothes over and over again because I had nothing else. I was living day by day. All I had was a broken, glass crack pipe and no one to turn to. I was homeless. Home was a drug-infested building for a day, a stranger's bed for a night or a room with multiple men. I had lost all sense of morality, common sense, and sound judgment. Truly, I was lost.

My confused state of mind kept me from being found or even reaching out for help. I was my own worst enemy, with no clue how deep I was falling or how I was going to get out of that nightmare. But did I really want to get out of it? The truth is, at the time I was perfectly content with not having a care in the world. I had no real responsibilities. My only commitment was to the crack pipe and finding the crack to go into it, by any means necessary. The fumes that altered my mind, hindered my sound judgment, and gave me the glooms, consumed me. I thought I needed the crack to live when in actuality it was killing me.

There is a verse in The Bible that many are familiar with, "Yea, though I walk through the valley of the shadow of death, I will fear no evil." – Psalms 23:4. Many people do not realize how dangerous the valley can be. In Biblical times, the sheep, cattle, and travelers would sometimes have to pass through the valley. They would constantly have to look over their shoulders, watching for danger, never knowing who will attack or when. While they were at the lowest, most vulnerable point, animals, robbers, and other prey would stake them out from a better vantage point and at the right time attack them, leaving them dead or helpless. I lived there for a long time, afraid, confused and thinking my pain and bondage was pleasure, believing I was free; but even when I thought I should have died, He protected me.

My hope is that my story will help bring someone out of his or her valley experience. It was not a time in my life that I am proud of, but I know that I am not the only one that has done some horrible things, fallen on hard times, and had feelings of defeat and despair or even a loss of hope. When it was time, when I was ready to answer His call, He pulled me out, cleaned me up, and set me on the path to showing others their truth, so that they too can be set free. Because of His love and grace, I am here today, no longer lost in the valley.

CHAPTER 1

A Purpose For Pain

Before I formed thee in the belly I knew thee; and before thou camest forth out of the womb I sanctified thee, and I ordained thee a prophet unto the nations. ~ Jeremiah 1:5

Nothing about me was ever ordinary. For starters, I am a triplet. I shared a womb with my sister and my brother. My sister and I are identical. In other words, our egg split, making us practically one and the same; meanwhile our brother is fraternal. He had his own egg, and he looks completely different from us. He resembles our dad more. Coincidentally, our mother had twins one year before having us triplets. Unfortunately, a few weeks after birth, one of them died due to an infection in his respiratory system, which wasn't uncommon back then. Prior to the twins my sister Margaret was born, the only single birth my mother had. In a time when the odds for spontaneous twin births were one in 55 and triplet births were far more uncommon at one in 3,323, the chances of the three of us being conceived, born, and surviving a fetal loss rate of 40% were slim, but we did.

We were raised in the projects on the north side of Bethlehem, Pennsylvania. All the houses looked exactly the same, with the red brick exterior. The only differences between them were the furniture people put in them and the flowers some people would have outside to try and make their house feel like a home, but it was still the projects. Outside you could typically find the setting of just about any low income, community in America.

It was in the projects that I came to understand and accept the mentality of the poor and impoverished. There is a saying that people fear what they don't understand, and hate what they can't conquer. I knew this all too well. We grew to be very tall and big. Most people in our schools and community couldn't look past our outward appearance and see our hearts. Like most children, we wanted so much to be liked and accepted. We just wanted to fit in, but our size intimidated most people, including our teachers. Instead we were feared. We were picked on, teased, and ridiculed because of our height and size. This provoked us to sometimes be the monsters that people perceived us to be. We were constantly fighting to protect each other and ourselves. We stood out, but we always stood together. Other kids saw us as bullies, though in actuality it was quite the opposite.

Because of our defensiveness at such an early age, we became protective of each other and developed defense mechanisms and coping skills. They were not the best, but in the mind of a child, they were sufficient. As time went on, we became more and more enraged because we were tired of being picked on and judged. Our mother was constantly being called to the school because of our behavior. We did our best to explain our side of the story, but people very seldom understood us. Our mother tried to pacify us as well as discipline us. We were going about things in the wrong way, but at the time it felt like the right thing to do. I can't recall us having many close friends because we didn't trust people easily. In our minds all we had was each other.

The most amazing person in all of this was my mother, Dilcy Mae Vereen. She nurtured and protected my siblings and I even when we misbehaved as children. My mother knew that it was more than our physical size that intimidated those that came in contact with us. She knew that we were special, different, and born with a purpose. She knew she needed to protect us when others tried to crush our will, and break our spirits. She knew why we survived and she knew her labor was not in vain. She didn't have much to give to us, but tried to show us a better way of living by her example and by giving us our first knowledge of God. She gave us a great foundation, and the wisdom she shared has been with me throughout my life and even in my darkest hours.

We saw the occasional fights and heard the occasional shootings, but in spite of it all, we felt safe. Our mother gave us curfews and wouldn't let us go too far, and she was always there. To say that this was a rough area of town would be an understatement. As a child I can remember seeing men and women on the corners—drug dealers selling drugs right in front of us, without even a second thought. I saw people fighting over drugs. Where there are drugs, there will always be a high crime rate, and that was the norm back then.

Life in the projects was very dangerous. Walking in the mornings to school was very scary because men would be out on the "hot corner" visibly selling drugs. This was the way of life in the projects, and to get through it we just kept our face forward, minded our own business, and walked straight to school.

I can remember instances of uncontrollable fear as a child, though eventually I was weaned of that fear as the environment became familiar and I began to feel invincible. One incident in particular I remember was when I was at Marvine Elementary. I was probably in the fourth grade. It was raining hard, and I put on my raincoat because we didn't have umbrellas. My sisters and brother had left me because I was running a bit behind. I was walking to school when I sensed someone trailing me. This was a drug-infested neighborhood with all sorts of criminals, so I turned and looked back and saw this man walking behind me. He was tall and thin, wearing a tan, three-quarter coat with a black umbrella. I remember the umbrella specifically because he used it to hide his face. I was terrified. I was alone and didn't want to get hurt. It was not uncommon for girls to be raped and taken advantage of. I wasn't a fool, so I began walking faster. As I walked faster, he increased his speed to match. I knew in my gut that something just wasn't right. My school was a long distance from where we lived, and we did not have a car. All my early elementary and middle school years, we had to walk to school, and it was at least two miles.

As the man walked toward me, one thought came to my mind: maybe I was just being paranoid and this man was walking fast to get out of the rain. I went back and forth with logic in my mind, but it just didn't make sense. Why was he still behind me? I thought there was no one else around; and if this man was going to try something, there was no one to help. I began to really get scared, and before I knew it, I was shaken with fear and couldn't do anything other than think of running, but I was too afraid. More doubts and questions were beginning to bombard my mind: What if I run? Will this man run after me and catch me? Then I heard a little voice in my head that said, "Run as fast as you can, and don't look back." Without another question or a second thought, I ran like I had fire under my feet, and I did not look back. I ran straight for the principal's office and told the principal what had happened. The principal said he would check it out and that I should go to class. I did not hear anything more about it. I never walked to school alone again at that age.

That was my earliest and one of my few memories of fear. Even though we were living in the valley of the shadow of death, I didn't quite know evil or fear it much. Our mother tried her best to shield us children and keep us in the house away from all harm and danger. She did her best with what she knew, and she was determined for us to survive.

We were raised on welfare, and this was all my mother knew at that time. Our family was very large, so they gave us two houses that were connected. We were the only family living in two houses with a room in between connecting them. We really only used one side, because we were seldom allowed to go into the other side. When my dad was around that's where he kept his friends and company. My mother tried very hard to prevent us from being exposed to our father's lifestyle. When we didn't have enough money, my mom found a way for us to live and be comfortable. If we didn't have enough food, she went to churches and food pantries to get food; and when we didn't have enough clothes, she went to the Salvation Army and other places to get us clothes. We never complained, because we saw just how hard she tried for us. She even worked at a food pantry once and got paid in food so that we would have enough. We never felt unloved or unwanted. In fact, she always kept us first. She was a great mother.

It didn't matter that we were not rich because our mother made us very comfortable there in the projects. Whatever we had, we were very grateful for. Our favorite meal she used to cook for us was pork chops, macaroni and cheese, and peas. It filled our little bellies. My sister Liana and I used to run and jump into our mother's bed, and she would let us. Her bed was like a bed of clouds; there was no better place in the house. Liana and I would eat so much it felt like our stomachs were ready to burst. Then we would have a contest to see who could make it to our mother's room the fastest after we were done eating. We were allowed to sleep in our mom's bed, and we did this so often we made a dent in the right side of the bed, and whichever one of us got there the fastest would plop her stomach right in the dent. These are the memories that I hold on to and cherish. We were safe, our bellies were full, and we had no worries.

Liana and I were best friends, and we began to fight other children in school to protect each other and ourselves. At the time we considered everyone else the enemy. We constantly got suspended from school for fighting. We rarely started a fight, but we never backed down from one. We were fighting often, but we were still kindhearted and loving to those who were kind to us. I thank my mother for the love she instilled in us. Because we were so loved, we knew how to give love.

I'm sure my mother could not understand or figure out our reason for being angry and fighting, but kids can be cruel. It hurt us deeply to be picked on and to be called an Amazon at such a young age. It hurt to be different because at the time I didn't understand why. Now as an adult, I learned how to turn that negative into a positive and I use it. In fact, I now welcome the name Amazon. Strength and power are positive traits of the Amazonian people. They are warriors. They have to be warriors to survive in the jungle. In hindsight, I was living my life in a jungle, a constant battleground. It was the fight and the strength that was instilled in me that allowed me to go on, not to mention the prayers from my mother and God's grace and mercy that kept me.

Our mother knew she needed help raising us right. She kept us in church as much as she could, we might not have gone every Sunday because we didn't own a car, but when mom got the thought to go nothing stopped her. We would even walk at times when we couldn't get a ride. It was during these walks when I realized that beautiful things existed in our community too. Mothers dressed their daughters like baby dolls with satin bows, ribbons and lace, and their boys like young men in miniature suits and ties. The women wore their Sunday best with beautiful hats, and smiling faces. Even the trees seemed bigger, the sun a little brighter, and the birds sang a little louder, beautiful songs of worship, preparing our hearts for joy. Everyone seemed kinder and more tolerant on a Sunday. We all shared a common hope and desire that things would get better, and we believed that they would. I knew then that there was a God, and that although things weren't perfect, He was always there.

We were very young when we first got baptized and got saved. At that time I believed getting baptized was the way to get saved, so I did it without the full understanding. It was what mom wanted and we just went with the flow of things. I don't recall feeling anything change or any feelings at all. As a child you imagine some kind of magical or special transformation right away. I later learned that a baptism is only an outward expression of an inward change, and not the other way around.

We went to many different churches because my mom never stopped searching for the perfect one, a church where she could feel like we belonged. At many of the churches that we attended we received rejection and ridicule from other children. We often wore clothes from different charity organizations and government assisted programs; although we were clean and neat, most of the items were dated or a little worn. This brought on unwanted attention, and we felt like we were not as good as the other children because they laughed at us and talked about us amongst themselves. It didn't matter to them that we were in church where we were supposed to be accepted and loved unconditionally.

When I was about eleven, there was one church in particular that we attended, probably the third church our mother took us to, and we desperately wanted to make friends. Naturally, we tried to befriend the pastor's daughter. She was very beautiful, and we assumed she was also nice. She had long hair, with shiny ribbons tied on each side. She wore the prettiest dresses and shoes even her socks were pretty. Although she was cute and smart, she was filled with hidden hatred and emotionally abused us. Behind the backs of the grown-ups she made us feel horrible. She would get with her other friends in the church and talk about us pointing and hinting with their eyes, they would laugh in our faces, and say mean things. This didn't help or lift up our already ruined self-esteem. It hurt to be rejected and unable to fit in once again. I know it hurt our mother when we would tell her we did not want to be there because of how the other kids made us feel and this resulted in us leaving to find another church. Our mother still did not have a full understanding of God, and her faith was still wavering, but she was trying. We saw how she asked questions seeking the truth trying to figure out the best route for our family as she often took the lead as mom and dad.

Mom was determined for us to go where we could fit in, I can remember a Jehovah's Witness coming by our house. They offered to help us. A lady would come by and pick us up and take us to their church, the Kingdom Hall. It was different and not at all what we were used to,

I don't recall seeing many other black families, but they were good to us. They helped us with clothes and rides to church, I can even remember them coming by on a Saturday, we all went to a park and then to a Bible study that they were having. It all seemed perfect. We were having fun and it didn't seem like anybody was judging us only helping us. I never knew why, but something must have been said that our mother didn't agree with because when they came around mom would tell us to be very quiet and to not open the door. Eventually, they stopped coming around and that was it for the Jehovah's Witnesses.

Our mother wanted us to go where they believed and taught the truth of Jesus Christ. Therefore she kept us in Baptist churches it wasn't until I got older that I found myself doing the very same thing, searching for a church to belong to, to fit in, to feel accepted and not rejected. I tried Methodist, Baptist, and others, but I finally settled in a Non-Denominational church with a Pentecostal background.

There was this young married couple, and I believe the husband was a youth pastor. They would go from house to house in the projects inviting us kids to church. This was perfect because they practically came to our front door. It was mostly about the children, and I don't recall our mom ever going with us, but she trusted the youth pastor and his wife enough to take us to church along with many of the other kids from the projects. It was a local church and they picked up children from both the Southside and the Northside of Bethlehem. When we arrived after a thirty-minute drive, we would see kids of all races and backgrounds, white, black, Asian and Hispanic. They made it fun for us; they gave us candy and were very kind. Although the candy was the motivating factor, we learned from their actions and example that Jesus is love. And they represented kindness.

This church was great for a while until my triplet sister and I started to misbehave and act out on the bus so much so that we got kicked off the bus and that was the end of that church. As we got older, my sister and I were terrible when it came to wanting attention, we didn't care if it was good or bad as long as the focus was on us. Years later, shockingly, that same church began to pick my children up from in front of our house.

* * * * * * *

I can't recall our dad ever coming to church with us, not once, that just wasn't his lifestyle. His life was in the streets. My dad was like a boss in the streets; he had many female friends, and lived the fast life that our mother tried so desperately to hide from us. My dad was a tall man, about six feet two inches, with the muscles of a bodybuilder. We obviously inherited his size and stature. He was incredibly handsome, and the women wanted him whether or not he was married. He abused both drugs and women and ultimately he let his love for both consume him. Watching my parents was not always the easiest thing to do. My dad was addicted to heroin and crack cocaine, which at that time seemed like a normal thing for people in the projects. She wanted him to clean up his life and be the man she knew he could be. She was so patient and forgiving of him, but there were times when, as children, we witnessed my parents fighting violently, because of his drug use.

He was also in and out of prison, but this seemed normal in our environment. There were a few times when we witnessed our mother calling the police on our dad during an argument and even times when my dad came home, and she refused to open the door. I understand where the hardening came from with my mom; she endured a lot, but never released it. She felt she had to be strong for us. She never wanted us to see her as weak as her situation made her feel.

Before my dad's downward spiral he would try to give my mother money but she refused it. It just didn't sit well with her. She tried to go along with it for a while, once she received a house full of brand new furniture. My dad tried to make up for not being there by offering her money, when what she really wanted was a family. After a while, she would rather go stand in the welfare line for free cheese and big blocks of butter, than sell her dreams of having a stable family for her children.

One day my dad came in with a stack of money and tried to give it to my mother. She was so fed up with the cheating and staying out that she didn't want it. They began to argue and the anger overtook her good judgment and she threw that money right back in his face. My dad lost it. They began to fight and in the struggle I can remember seeing mom hit the glass table in the kitchen. My heart was racing; as it shattered things seemed to slow down. I heard her scream for us to run out of the kitchen and go over to the neighbor's house. I was terrified, but I could only wonder if she was going to be okay. The fear that I had could not compare to the love and protection I felt for my mother. She did not want us to see the violence. It was always devastating to see them fight, but we were used to hearing them argue, and became numb to the noise. She wasn't physically hurt that day, but the pain, and humiliation she felt we couldn't see. It was eating away at her as she built up the courage and a plan to be independent so that we could leave the projects and the negative environment we were living in.

We never talked about it and after a while things just went back to the way they were, mom being both mom and dad when she had to. We still loved our dad unconditionally he was still daddy and our mother raised us to honor him in spite of the lifestyle he lived. The drugs took a serious toll on their marriage and his life. Our mother saw how monstrous the disease of addiction really was. I saw how it affected him and the people around him. I often wondered how he could choose this thing over his own flesh and blood. I would never have thought that I would find out first hand, years later.

When our mother walked away from the projects and government assistance she was tired; tired of them being in her business, tired of the hold the system had on her and her progress. Being in that system also contributed to our dad not being there a good portion of the time. Even though they were legally married, he was not allowed to be there because he was not on the lease. I'm sure if my dad suggested for us to move, and proved that he would support all of us she would have done it in a heartbeat, but my dad was torn. His mind was in too many places at one time. Drug abuse and that fast life kept him lost, unable to find reality.

It was my mother that said it is better to struggle with a little dignity than to have more and struggle with more bondage. She left it, walked away and because of this I believe she saved us. We still had our paths and journeys to walk, but she made it a bit easier by showing us it can be done.

After we left the projects she finally submitted and surrendered all to Christ around the age of 36. It was a gradual process but she began to take us to church more and more and you could finally see the faith, courage and strength that was building on the inside being reflected on the outside. Her dressing began to change, her confidence was evident, and you just knew she was a different person. I drew from her strength years later when I needed the courage to walk away from the lifestyle that was killing me. There was a purpose for the pain after all. My mother died in 2002; may she rest in peace.

CHAPTER 2

Innocence Lost

Jesus said, "Let the little children come to me, and do not hinder them, for the kingdom of heaven belongs to such as these." ~ Matthew 19:14

There is a special innocence in childhood, and when it is taken away or disrupted, it can never be replaced. When your innocence and virtue are robbed from you, mental, emotional, and psychological anguish will surface. For some it surfaces immediately. For others it sits beneath the surface and quietly waits for opportunities to destroy your life. It breaks through under the guise of fits of rage, unhealthy habits, substance abuse, dysfunctional relationships, and other destructive behavior. Not long did I live in a daydream of butterflies and fairies. These dreams of fantasy were replaced quickly with nightmares of abuse, separation and insanity. Many traumatic events caused me to lose hope in people, safety, and security. Events that opened doors to knowledge that I was too young to understand and did not swiftly recover from. I spent years searching for quick fixes trying to undo the damage left behind, mostly just wanting to forget and numb the pain.

At the age of seven, my older cousin molested me. I was completely unaware of what sex was or what it even meant when it was spoken about. I just had no idea. At seven all I was thinking about was food and dolls and not much more than that. I was an innocent little child just wanting to be a kid.

My mother went out with her sister one day and left one of our older cousins in charge to babysit us. She thought he was old enough to look after us. He had never proven to be untrustworthy and never gave my mother or aunt any reason to think otherwise. As soon as my mom and aunt left, he didn't waste any time in executing his plan. He put each of us in different rooms of the house, trying to make us take a nap.

I remember that it was a bright and sunny day. At seven, life is simple, and you only think about the simpler things like toys, having fun, playing games with friends and eating too much candy. "Let's play a game," he suggested, walking into the room. I had on a little yellow full-body suit that snapped between the legs. "Lay down," he said. I was wondering what kind of game we were going to play lying down. I can remember him standing there in front of me with his zipper opened and his pants unbuttoned. "Put it in your mouth." he demanded. I was confused and beginning to feel uncomfortable, but still waiting for the game. There was the most horrible smell, and I hesitated. He held his penis and urged me forward. I didn't understand it at the time, because I really thought we were going to play a game, totally unaware that it was going to be a "game" that would destroy my innocence.

He was making us go to sleep, so I thought that if we were going to play a game I didn't have to sleep. I began to feel terror and confusion. This felt wrong, dirty and disgusting, and I still didn't understand what was happening. Even if this was a game I just wanted it to stop. Shortly thereafter he stopped and went to check on everyone. There were at least three different bedrooms with children in each of the separate rooms. While he was out checking on my brother and sisters, I just stayed there, too scared to move and feeling really uncomfortable and confused. He came back in and said, "This is our secret." then left me alone with so many questions and feelings.

At seven, I just didn't know what to do, and I didn't even understand what had taken place. I just knew it felt wrong, and I tried to forget about it. I didn't tell anyone after it happened, but as I got a little older the memory and confusion resurfaced. I wanted to know and understand why my older cousin did this to me.

It finally came out one day when we were all at my aunt's house, and my mother was in the kitchen. I thought it was the perfect time. I had to tell, because it began to drive me crazy. I took the opportunity and told my mom and my cousin's mom at the same time. My mother cried. She was in disbelief. My cousin was not in the house at the time, so they weren't able to question him. My cousin was sick, and he may have been molested himself. I am not sure whether his mother said anything to him about it. I do know that when my sister Margaret found out about it, she lost it. She chased him down with a stick and beat him like he stole something, which he did. He survived, but he never touched me again. Our mother didn't leave us alone with anybody else ever again.

When I was about ten years old, my mother went through some

changes in her life. She was very busy taking care of us children, cooking, cleaning, and trying to maintain a safe environment for us while trying to keep up with my dad. She began taking diet pills so she could look and feel better. My mother was a very beautiful woman, and in my opinion she didn't need to lose weight. But she was married to my dad, who was very handsome and women were constantly throwing themselves on him. She had competition and her self-esteem and confidence needed a little boost. Love is supposed to be unconditional, but my mother began feeling lonely because of my dad's behavior and lifestyle. She wanted to believe that if she changed her appearance, their marriage would improve. This was not the case. When a person is addicted to drugs, there's not much anyone can do to keep the addict's attention. She may have thought it was her appearance when in actuality, an addict is an addict until he or she wants to change, is in recovery and on the way to deliverance. Up until then, the focus is on the addiction, and nothing will distract the addict from it.

It was during this time that people believed my mother was losing her mind because of the explosive mood swings and depressed states she displayed. As a result of this, someone close to her had her committed to the psychiatric unit at the hospital. It's easy to see why someone on the outside looking in might think my mom had a severe mental condition. If I can get straight to the point, my mother was with the five of us small children, day in and day out with no break and no one to ease her load. We were her sole responsibility. We didn't have the support of our extended family, and that coupled with my father's lifestyle, addictions, rejection and the heartache she felt constantly, its no wonder she had a nervous breakdown. There was no real foundation; there was nothing for her to stand on, and when she would pull away from the church and God, things got worse.

When the ambulance came and the attendants strapped her down onto a bed, it was a nightmare. I watched my mother cry and scream, trying to fight them off, but she was outnumbered and they were determined. There was nothing we could do and all of the adults just stood around looking. I didn't understand what was going on, why was no one helping her? I was angry and upset because I knew my mother was not crazy, and she was all we really had. She may have been depressed, but she was the only thing stable in our lives. She loved us unconditionally and showed us that every second of her life. How could these people come in to steal us from our mother, the only one we had to protect us! Despite everything that was going on, I never judged her and I knew that what was going on was not her fault.

They took her off to the hospital and the social workers gathered us kids up and took us to separate places. For the moment my mother had lost total control over her life and ours, and the state was now dictating where we should live and with whom we should live. This was against everything our mother believed in, but there wasn't much she could do, other than to get better so we could go back home.

As a child going through this kind of crisis, you feel intense emotion that could either break you or teach you coping mechanisms that stick with you throughout your life. I was numb, and forced myself not to feel the pain or acknowledge that my mother was gone. That was how I got through this period. I had a lot of questions but just continued to go with the flow of things hoping things would get better and we would be reunited with our mom. I don't know where our dad was in that moment, but it was all a mess, a nightmare that I kept hoping to wake up from.

There was no one that we knew who was able to take care of us. I can't recall what was going on with my aunts at that time, but we were all split up and put in different foster homes. They kept my triplet sister Liana, and I together. Through all of this, I was very angry, and I began to feel some bitterness; I was mad at the world. When they separated Liana and me from our other siblings, my anger, confusion and fear intensified. I didn't know if we were ever going back home or if we were ever going to be a family again.

We were later placed in the care of the Brookes. This particular family did this sort of thing for a living. They took in foster children and got paid by the state to care for them. They were not required to show us love, teach us good values, or be role models. This was why we did not feel loved while we were there. Mrs. Brookes would physically fight my sister on a regular basis. Because we were so big, she probably did not see anything wrong with it. My sister was already angrier than I, so she always fought back. At night Mr. Brookes would open the door to my room and just look in. It did not feel right; it felt eerie. When I heard that door open, I immediately pretended to be asleep.

It felt like he was plotting, getting ready to go in for the kill.

Mr. Brookes had a red recliner that was turned in a way where no one would be able to see around it. If you were sitting on the couch you couldn't see around the chair. One day, while we were watching a movie, he called me to sit on the chair next to him. I thought I was in trouble, so I went humbly and sat down. He started rubbing my leg and put his fingers in my panties. I was shocked, and some of the feelings I had when my cousin violated me, resurfaced. I was terrified, and started to feel very uncomfortable. I knew that he should not be doing that. I was angry but I felt hopeless. I thought, "Why is this nasty, old, dirty man doing this?" I hated it, and he just kept on playing in my private area until he heard Mrs. Brookes coming, then he stopped. So I just stayed there. I didn't know what else to do. I had seen her fights with my sister and I didn't want to get into trouble. Later that night he came to the room, opened the door, and peeked in. Again, I acted as if I was sleeping. It was obvious why he came to my room every night. My instincts and feelings were correct. He was waiting for the perfect opportunity to get me. I didn't understand prayer, but my soul cried out for help, and I knew God heard my cry. Within the next few days, we were told that we were going to be returned to our mother. It was around Christmas time, and Mr. Brookes pulled me aside and said to me, "If you stay, I will buy you a bike." He just didn't know that even as a ten-year-old, I was not stupid. There was no amount of money or gifts in the world that would have made me want to stay at that house. I wanted to go home.

The social worker came and picked us up and returned us to our mother, where we belonged. The nightmare was over; I was safe again. I didn't tell anyone immediately what had happened to me. I just wanted to forget it. After all, it was Christmas, and I just didn't want to hurt my mother or give her anything more to stress about. The important thing was that we were home. There were decorations everywhere, and there were so many gifts under the tree for all of us. We were together again, and we were all happy. I just wanted to enjoy it. Later I found out that our dad went and signed our mother out of the hospital and demanded that they gather us kids back up and bring us all back home.

Nothing like that incident in the foster home ever happened again in my youth. It wasn't until later, in adulthood, that I even mentioned anything about that incident. I just wanted to forget it and move on, not knowing that while I was trying to forget it and move on I was building scars on the inside. I was often confused about things, I felt a lot of fear and insecurity; the trauma of these situations caused me to constantly seek out external things to comfort me and quiet my internal conflict.

* * * * * * *

Although I was safe in my mother's care, I didn't feel secure anymore. I realized that I had very little control, and very little power. I wasn't given the right tools to recover from the traumas I had faced, so I found my own. Food was my first addiction. I found a comfort in food and abused its power. I ignored the side effects of overeating and watched myself become overweight, shielded by new layers of protection. I didn't realize that being overweight made me feel even more insecure, and even more out of control, which caused me to eat more. It was a horrible cycle that damaged my self-esteem.

Low self-esteem causes insecurity, depression, and desperation. No one really wants to admit he or she suffers from low self-esteem, but I did. At the time I didn't know low self-esteem was the issue, or what was causing it. As a child and teenager you usually don't know when you have something emotionally or psychologically wrong, and when confronted with it, denial often sets in. We want to see ourselves as strong and confident, but sometimes that is not the case. I wish I knew what was happening to me, or how to address it with my mom, or even someone to show me a better way of coping with my internal fears.

I often displayed over-the-top behavior. My insecurities caused me to crave attention, whether good or bad, this was also an addiction. I did whatever it took, not caring about my reputation or the consequences. This addiction led me to make very bad choices including the way I dressed, and the way I carried myself. I found myself trying desperately to fit in with other people. It didn't matter if what they were doing was right or wrong; I just wanted to belong. I latched on to anyone who was willing to show me love or attention no matter what I had to do to get it. Had I been more secure with myself, I never would have allowed men to treat me in an abusive manner. But how could they value me when I didn't even know how to value and love myself? I found myself constantly, but unknowingly, looking for approval, confirmation, and validation from people. After dealing with so much rejection as a child, I couldn't handle it. I needed people to love me, at any cost. I constantly gave in to peer-pressure which steered me down a dark path from my teens into adulthood.

Eventually I settled into abusive relationships that nearly cost me my life. I wanted to be loved and accepted so badly, but I believed I was unworthy to be loved for who I was. I knew I was too young to be in a committed relationship with a man who was twenty-one years old and I was just fourteen, but I was so desperate to be wanted, loved, and accepted that when he came along, I blocked out any concerns about age and morals. I thought this man loved me, and I truly made him my world because he acted like I was his. I was wrong! He preyed on my insecurity, immaturity, vulnerability, and desperation for love and attention. In return he took whatever remaining innocence I had left.

CHAPTER 3

He Loves Me, He Loves Me Not

The hunger for love is much more difficult to remove than the hunger for bread.
~ Mother Teresa

Time had passed. It was a new year, I was fourteen years old, and in the ninth grade. I was still acting up, but now that anger was turning into rebellion. It was then that I met a guy we called Ice. I was still feeling like nobody accepted me or even noticed me, and I was not feeling attractive either. Ice showed interest in me at a time when I needed attention. I was so amazed and surprised when he told me I was pretty, this made me pay attention to him, looking for him everyday after school. He was always there, and naturally I thought he was a student. I soon found out that he was twenty-one years old, and he did not attend our school. Initially this was shocking, and I knew my mother would never approve, but he was interested in me and I pretended like it didn't matter.

Fathers do not understand the power that they have to change the future of their daughters. I don't blame my father for the paths that I chose, but I can't help but wonder if he was around more to tell me how beautiful or special I was, would I have been so amazed to hear it from a man. I didn't know my worth, or even that I was valuable at all. Dads boost their daughter's self-esteem in a way that mothers cannot. Without a healthy relationship from positive male and female influences, girls are doomed to make poor choices in the areas of love.

Ice made me feel special, wanted, and appreciated, and I couldn't believe this guy wanted to be with me. Yes, my mom loved me, but this was different. Like other girls my age, I wanted a boyfriend and I began to date this twenty-one-year-old man. Soon I didn't think about his age at all, only the way he made me feel when we were together. He would come up every day after school to see me, would kiss and hold hands. I was so proud to finally have a boyfriend like the other girls. I thought it was love. I started leaving my house to walk back to the projects without my mother's permission or knowledge. He lived in those very projects that my mother worked so hard to remove us from. I knew better, but I didn't care about any consequences. I just knew he made me feel good.

Things began to escalate with a little more kissing and a lot more time together. I would walk across town just to see him. I had to see him. I thought he was my world. We began to have some alone time, just the two of us in the room. I was not at all experienced, not in relationships and not in life for that matter. I was only fourteen. He began to touch me, but this touching I wanted because I believed he wanted me and he loved me. He then began to give me oral sex. This feeling was very different and made me feel like I wanted to go farther—and we did. One day he was down there and looked at me and said if I would let him put it in me, it would feel even better. I believed this man loved me and would marry me because of how he was making me feel, and all I wanted was him. However, when he entered me, it didn't feel good at all. Though he was gentle, it hurt, and I bled. I became afraid, but he said it was normal, and he comforted me.

As time went on, my mother began to notice changes in my behavior. Curious about what I had been up to, she found out pieces of information and put it all together. She discovered the guy I was seeing was a grown man who had no business dating a girl my age. I didn't care because he was the only guy that paid attention to me in that way. I didn't have to allow things to happen, but they did. He made me feel like I was in control, but in reality, I had none. He was controlling my mind and my actions, like a puppet on a string.

Ice and I never used condoms. This was my first experience with a guy, so I didn't think anything of it. I thought I was so in love with him that nothing could deter me from wanting him. He told me shortly after we started dating that he got into a fight with some guys who were jumping his brother and while trying to help his brother he got some of his brother's blood all over his body. He mentioned that he had some cuts along the sides of his fingers. His hands were so dried that they cracked, leaving openings in his skin. I didn't understand what that had to do with me and why he was telling me that. He said, "Because my brother has AIDS." Being as young, ignorant, naive, and desperate as I was, it didn't dawn on me that he was trying to tell me he might have been infected with AIDS.

Eventually, my mother threatened to call the police and have him arrested. I couldn't understand why she didn't want me to be happy. I later understood that she was just doing her job as my mother. I was so wrong. I was too young for a twenty-one-year-old man. I was too young for sex. I was too young for all the changes I allowed myself to endure. But as my mother often said, "If you can't hear, you will feel."

Although my dad had his own issues that he was struggling with, my mother still spoke with him and tried to make him feel like he was included in our lives. She told my dad about what was going on between Ice and I. My dad must have spoken to him, because not long after, we stopped seeing each other. I went over one last time to see him, and the people he lived with told me he was in jail. I knew they were lying. My dad probably threatened him. In spite of my father's addiction to drugs he still had a "bad boy" reputation. People knew that my father didn't play around especially when it came to his money and his children. I believe this was why Ice got scared and backed off, and that was the end of that season. I thank God that I didn't get pregnant or contract a disease in my rebellion and ignorance.

* * * * * * *

I wanted to be loved, even if it meant compromising the truth, the morals, and the values my mother tried to instill in me while I was growing up. When I first met Scott Price, he was the nicest—not to mention the cutest—guy in the world to me. My oldest sister, Margaret, had some friends that would come over to the house while our mom was at work. Sometimes they would just pick her up, other times they would stick around for a little. One of her friends who came by was Scott; he was very handsome and charismatic. He immediately made an impression on me.

After dating an older man, and having sex at such an early age, I thought I was mature. My confidence had gone through the roof, even though it was a false confidence and in all the wrong things, I was really into myself. I had outgrown the baby fat and was looking good. My self-esteem was through the roof. I had blossomed into a beautiful young adult. I was tall and thin and many guys showed me attention and expressed how beautiful I was. That validation even made me a little conceited. One day in particular, I was dressed in a cute pair of shorts with a half shirt to match. I was walking home from the grocery store, when Scott stopped and offered to take me home; so I got into the van, which belonged to his mom. As he was taking me home, it gave us some time to talk alone.

Scott was mixed with both a black and a white parent. He was tall and his skin was the color of creamy caramel. He had a muscular build; a well defined six pack, and big feet. He had the cutest brown eyes, and when the sun hit his eyes, they were like honey. He had beautiful curly hair, and in my opinion he was perfect. I was impressed with his appearance and he was only four years older than I was. I always had a tendency to move too fast; I wanted him. I was in this guy's van, imagining us together and before I got out, I had it in my mind that this guy was going to be my boyfriend. What I didn't know was that he was thinking the same thing.

I didn't know much about him, but I knew he was going to be mine. As time went on, I would see Scott popping up in our neighborhood more frequently. He always knew when to come, perhaps because the only time he could come was when my mom was at work. My mother was very protective but for good reasons. I was fifteen, about to turn sixteen, feeling cute, looking cute, and now this cute guy was going to be mine. Things couldn't be better.

I started talking about him around the house more and more, until I finally built up the nerve to tell Mom about him. I was really starting to like him, and I loved to watch him walk. He had these straight legs with a bit of a bow curve to them. He looked so good, especially when he cleaned up. I thought the difference between then and when I was fourteen was that I knew it all. In actuality, I didn't know much about anything.

All I was interested in was looking good for Scott. My mom knew I was more serious about him than any other guy before. All I spoke about was Scott; I was obsessed, and there was no middle ground for me. It was all or nothing. Either you were mine, or you were not. I wasn't interested in dating and then later let's take time to see where it goes. No way! I was an impulsive, fast paced teenager.

I had learned the art of seduction, I observed what made men want me. What got their attention, and what made them pursue me. I decided it was time to turn on the charm and lock down this relationship once and for all. I had a routine and style for my make up, hair, and clothes; it centered on being sexy, and seductive. My eyes were like cat's eyes. I wore gray contact lenses with heavy black eyeliner, to complement my eyes. I would line my eyes to appear like the shape of cat's eyes. I had long blonde braid extensions and I wore red lipstick. This was the routine I did right before I saw him, and he wasn't going to be able to tell me no. When he saw me, his eyes lit up with approval. I figured a direct approach would be best, and I said to him, "So, what are we doing? Are you trying to be mine or not?" I knew I startled him, but he couldn't resist. He said Okay, and then I said Okay, and it was official.

We began to hang out a lot. We became very close and we were inseparable. It was rare to see me without him and vice versa. Then Margaret saw us together, and she asked me what I was doing with him. I said, "He's my man. Why?" She gave me a questionable look, as if to ask if I was serious. And, yes, I was very serious. I was developing some immense feelings for Scott. To me he was the perfect gentleman. We held hands everywhere, and when he couldn't get his mom's car, he walked from Allentown to Bethlehem or rode a bike to come see me. I believed that he was dedicated to me and surely must be the one I was going to marry.

Margaret didn't say much. She did say that he was her friend, and my next question was, "Did you have sex with him?" She said, "No," and I was relieved because sex sealed the deal for me. I told her that I really did like him, and she said, "OK" and walked away. I was still puzzled by the look she left with, but I was happy because I could be with him. Had my sister said they did have sex or that they were going together, I would have let it go and looked for another boyfriend. I didn't believe in being with a man that one of my sisters had already been with.

So Margaret walked away, and so did I, just as happy as I could be because now I knew Scott with his fine self was mine and nobody was going to stop it—nobody. My mother started to like Scott because he was so respectful and soft-spoken toward her. I was glad for that because if he got on my mom's bad side, there was no way things were going to work out for us. Mom had a temper at times and we did our best to avoid conflict with her.

Scott and I began to hang out more at his house. His mom was cool. She drank like a fish and was always drunk, but she still loved me, and I respected and loved her too. When it was getting late, she would make Scott take me home. Linda was awesome to be around. She was like one of the people we hung out with. When Linda would go out, she would leave Scott and me in her air-conditioned room to lie in her bed and watch movies. This was so much fun. She didn't do much grocery shopping for the house, but she did a lot of food shopping for her room. It was where all the goodies were—cookies, cakes, chips, soda, a bunch of junk—and when she permitted us, we were in there devouring them, and she didn't mind.

At other times we would hang out together at Scott's other friends' houses. They lived up in the nearby projects (low-income housing) called the Units, and we would hang out with his boys. He kept me close as if I wanted to cheat. Scott just didn't know he was all I wanted at the time and I could never have eyes for another because of how full my eyes were with him. We met up with some of his other friends who were a few years older than he was. I was no stranger to drinking beer. I was even smoking cigarettes. But then Scott started going a bit overboard with the drinking to the point he would vomit. This was not cute. But later, after I cleaned up his vomit, he would say he wouldn't drink like that again, and I would believe him because I was really starting to feel some love for him.

Scott introduced me to many things. From him I received passion, and I had never really experienced that before. I spent many nights in his home where he would hold me and I felt loved, wanted and needed. He had his own room, which faced the front of the house. His was the typical male room. It was painted a light blue color. It had one tall dresser, a small closet and a full-sized bed that was pushed up against the wall on the right side of the room. The dresser was at the front of the room so that as you opened the door and looked to the right, there was the tall dresser. The closet was on the left side of the room, and far back were three bay windows. This became my home away from home. I began to make up stories to tell my mom so that I could sleep over. A few times I told my mom I was stranded, which, in fact, I was because

Linda had come in drunk and stumbling all over the place and had hidden the keys so Scott couldn't take the car, so much for her being in agreement with him to make sure I got home. Eventually, after staying out as much as I did, my mother no longer got upset with me. She knew I was with Scott and that I was safe. I was well past sixteen by then, and really thinking I was grown and could do what I wanted. My mother didn't have the strength or time to fight with me. She hoped that the seeds she planted were good enough and trusted that I would make the right choices. I needed guidance, but I was not going to listen to what others had to say, even if it was for my good. I wanted to learn by experience not fully aware or ready to deal with all of the consequences. I was going to be with Scott, and that was the bottom line.

After about a year of being with Scott, things started to change. His behavior started to worsen. In public he was still as sweet as pie, but behind closed doors he was changing into something evil. He became very controlling, and it was starting to be too much. When I mentioned my concern about his behavior, he would apologize and tell me he was still dealing with issues from his father's death; and I would forgive him.

We made love like we were already married, and I dreamed that one day I would be his wife. We would be the perfect couple with beautiful children and live happily ever after. Then one day, while we were having a good time at his house, listening to music as we often did, out of nowhere he started crying and saying I could never leave him. I was shocked and confused. He frightened me because there was something dark in his tone and his eyes. I did love him, but the things coming out of his mouth were psychotic. Once again he blamed it on his past issues and drinking, and said it would not happen again. I was young, in love and very naïve. I wanted to believe that he could change and be better. In many ways I believed I could achieve what my mother was never able to achieve with my father. I thought I could fix a broken boy as if he were a toy, make him love me, and choose me over his demons. I was a little girl playing grown up games. Little did I know, this was only the beginning and the worst was yet to come.

CHAPTER 4
The Beginning of the End

And when the woman saw that the tree was good for food, and that it was pleasant to the eyes, and a tree to be desired to make one wise, she took of the fruit thereof, and did eat, and gave also unto her husband with her; and he did eat. ~ Genesis 3:6

I was still going to school, but it was not as important to me. I did enough to get by, but my focus was not there. I knew it would be good if I graduated, but I had convinced myself that Scott was my backup plan. Certainly, we were going to get married and take care of each other. Many people in my environment didn't finish high school, but at least they were able to get a job or get a good hustle going where they made enough to survive. I knew my mother wanted me, and all of her children, to finish high school at the very least. My older sister, Buffy, had already dropped out of high school, so to appease our mother, I continued. I didn't want her to blame Scott and break us apart. I was content and living day by day. I was happy as long as I was with Scott. Then suddenly, quickly and almost without any warning, it all changed.

Early one morning, I was over at Scott's house having some cereal, and things were going well. Then all of a sudden, Scott brought some things to the table after breakfast. As if he was getting ready to bake a cake he placed a spoon, baking soda, a pipe, and a little plastic bag, with a white substance in it, on the table. I was thinking, "What the heck is this?" and then the bombshell hit: this man was getting ready to do some drugs right in front of me! There was the man that I was so proud to claim as my perfect boyfriend, the man I knew I was going to marry one day! I watched him pour the white, powdery substance out onto the spoon, and then he took some baking soda and placed some on the spoon and then added water and then lit some matches underneath it. As I watched, so many questions began to flash through my mind. It wasn't very becoming at all, and it certainly wasn't cute, but I sat silently and watched because I loved him. As I stared in disbelief, the admiration I once felt for him was beginning to melt away. He took a penny and played with the substance until it became hard on the penny. Then he put it on a paper towel to dry. He soon took the pipe, put a piece of the hardened substance on the tip, and put the pipe to my mouth. He told me to inhale as he lit a flame. I was terrified but curious. I couldn't trust myself because of the internal conflict I was facing. I didn't know what I was going to do, or what was going to happen. I tried to be strong and said no, but he said that it wouldn't hurt me. I knew there would be no immediate pain, but I knew the dangers and consequences of using drugs very well. Eventually, reluctantly, I gave in. I didn't do it right with the first light, so he showed me how to do it and lit it again. That was the very first time I smoked cocaine.

It was like someone showing you how to play cards or checkers. That was how the love of my life showed me how to smoke cocaine. After I inhaled correctly and blew it out, it was like no feeling I ever felt before. At that very moment, everything my mother had taught me, everything I had witnessed in my past, went straight out of the window. All the times I heard my mother screaming at my dad because of his drug use, all my past determination to avoid using cocaine—I forgot it all. I liked it because he liked it; and if it was good for him, it had to be good for me. We sat there and smoked up all that he had that morning, and when it was gone we had sex; there was nothing more to do.

When I got some time to myself, I tried desperately to process what had happened, and I couldn't believe what I had done. I kept it to myself. Neither my sister Liana nor my mother knew. But I understood why Margaret gave me that look, as she was walking away. She must have known Scott did drugs, but I was naïve and knew nothing of his drug habits. All I knew was that I just wanted to be loved and accepted by my man. I was even a little bit pleased that he trusted me enough to share his secrets with, that he thought I was mature enough to handle it. It was as if our relationship was going to another level. I didn't realize that it was a level in the wrong direction.

Some time went by, and neither of us spoke about it again. We went on like nothing had happened. We went back to drinking as usual, but now I wondered about something else: now that we had smoked cocaine, was this thing going to continue? Eventually, it did. We began sniffing cocaine each time we drank on a regular basis, like dessert after a good meal. Scott had a friend named Chris, and would go to his basement and drink some 40 ounce bottles of Old English and Colt 45 and chill. Soon Chris would pull out the cocaine and Scott would get this look in his eyes like it was a treat, like cake and cookies. I knew he loved it more than he loved me, just as my father chose it over his family. I was thinking I was in way too deep, but I couldn't leave my boyfriend all alone; he needed me. Lying to myself was easier than accepting that I was making the same mistakes my mother did. I wish I could have seen the path I was headed down and the destruction I was bringing on myself, but only hindsight is 20/20, and I was just a kid.

Scott's behavior was getting stranger by the day. He would leave me at home in his room while he went out. I knew he was going to get high, and it was happening on a regular basis. After being out practically all night, he would come back and wake me up wanting to argue. My only crime was sleeping over at his place. He came back only when the drugs ran out and along with them his patience.

Once we got past that, morning came, and he sobered up and acted as if nothing had happened. No one knew for a while, but I had started lying to everyone about Scott because he was supposed to be my perfect boyfriend. I had totally left my family —my triplet sister Liana, my mom, my other siblings, everybody.

Time passed and things were pretty calm in the house for a while. I was still in Allentown staying with Scott and his mom; I practically lived there. We had cooled off of the drinking for a while and stayed in watching television and communicating a lot more; mostly because we had no money to buy alcohol or drugs. Scott was unemployed and had a hard time keeping a job. His mother was becoming impatient with him and for good reason. He was a twenty-year-old man, and he had no ambition. His ambition in life was me, and my ambition was him; we were in love.

We couldn't live on love alone. His mom was trying, but her drinking was becoming uncontrollable. After her husband died, the order and structure in their family died too. Bills were mounting, there was no food, the phone was turned off, and things were spinning out of control. Scott got up one morning and asked his mom if he could borrow the car because he and his friend were going to go job hunting. The van had stopped working, so she got another car, a little yellow Rabbit that had two doors, and was great on gas. When anybody had money to put gas in the tank, which wasn't too often, we were able to use it.

There were times when Scott would try to hustle up $2 to put gas in the tank because when his mom got really drunk, she would make me go home. She was right, but it was a bit too late. I had already been exposed to a dysfunctional lifestyle, and I liked it as long as I could be with Scott.

At one point I was home at my mom's house, but it didn't feel like home because Scott couldn't be there with me. I was missing Scott so much I couldn't take it anymore, so I caught the bus to his house. I didn't work, and neither did Scott, so he slept in often. When Scott got a job, it would only last for about two weeks—long enough to get paid—and that was it; on to the next job, after a couple of months. When I got there, Scott was sleeping. His mother opened the door for me. This particular morning he was so happy to see me it was as if we hadn't seen each other for a year, when it had been only about a week. Scott and I were always together, but things were getting out of hand.

We were out, and one of his boys told him I had been trying to get at him, which was a lie. I never cheated on Scott, nor did I desire another man. Scott confronted me with his fist. I was stunned but not surprised. After all the erratic behavior he was displaying, this was the one thing I was anticipating. I had seen this scene play out before, but I was much younger, and I was not the victim, my mother was. He hit me so hard that I saw different colored lights due to the impact of the blow. My eye swelled and was blackened. I definitely couldn't go back to my mom's for a while.

I had never been hit like that in my life. I cried, and cried, but not just because of the pain. I couldn't believe what was happening to me. I thought of the sad pathetic life I was living and saw a glimpse of my future. I cried because I knew I didn't have the strength to leave him in that moment. Even though he hit me, all I could think of was how much I needed him. Like a drug, more than the cocaine, more than the alcohol, I needed him to love me, and I believed that I wouldn't be able to survive without him. I could survive the blow that blackened my eye, the pain and scars would soon go away, but the pain of a broken heart was too much to even imagine.

Once I could catch my breath, I asked him why he did it, and he said it was because his boy said I was trying to get at him. I told him that he didn't have any proof and that it was wrong to hit me for hearsay without even finding out if there is any truth to it. He saw that I was very angry, and I told him that I was not going to put up with it, that I was better than that. But who was I fooling? It worked in the moment, because when he thought I was getting ready to break up with him, he dropped to his knees and begged me not to leave him. Sobbing, he told me I was the best thing that ever happened to him and he couldn't live without me. And I needed to hear that. I needed to believe that he did love me, that it was real love after all. It was the next level in our relationship, once again in the wrong direction.

We cried together and comforted each other, but I was the one sitting there with the black eye. He appeared to be so sorry. It seemed genuine, so I stayed, and we cried each other to sleep, wrapped in each other's arms. There it was. I was hooked again, hooked on his affection and attention and how he made me feel wanted and needed.

Days went by, and everything was going well and everyone was happy. So I called my mom from time to time to let her know I was fine and everything was good. Then one night Linda came in drunk with some black man. Linda was white, but she only dated black men. I never saw her with any other race of people. So she came in with the guy, and they were both drunk. They went straight up to her room, and Scott followed them while I stayed downstairs in his room. When Scott came back down, he had that excited look in his eyes, and I knew what it meant. Not only was Scott getting high, but also his mom and the man she had up there with her. Here we go again, I thought, but I joined him, and we got high. This time he got enough for us to stay up the whole night. He kept going back and forth from his mom's room and then down to where I was, getting the drugs from upstairs.

What a life. I was sixteen years old in an abusive, dysfunctional, drug-addicted relationship. When Scott got started, forget it; but when he was clean there was no talk of it, he was my perfect boyfriend who just couldn't keep a job. These were all negatives that I tried to dress up as a positive by making excuses for everything he was doing as long as he kept on loving me.

I just couldn't see that it was all wrong, or maybe I didn't want to see it at the time. There were many nights of drug use—up all-night and sleeping all day. This lifestyle was not conducive to high school and going was not even something I seriously considered anymore. When I wasn't high, I sometimes thought of what it would mean for my future if I didn't graduate and felt some guilt and regret. That would motivate me to go for a day or two. My attendance was definitely dropping and so were my chances to fix my future. Scott didn't encourage me to go, because that meant that I wouldn't be with him all day, but he didn't discourage me if I made up my mind to go on any given day.

One day we began to get high with Scott's mother. We were all sitting in the kitchen—me, Scott, Linda, and another woman, who was a prostitute with no place to stay. This woman had on a wild wig, tight, light blue jeans and a low-cut black top. I began to observe a few things. She only was able to stay until her drugs ran out, but when her drugs got smoked up, she had to go. She had a foul odor that smelled like a dead, rotten fish. I wondered if she knew. I believe she did but dismissed it because all she wanted to do was sit there and get high. But the smell was raw. It was probably a terrible bacterial infection that she ignored because of the drug use. What surprised me was that no one was interested in food or bathing, only in getting high. No one wanted to move from the table, all of us sat there, waiting for the next hit. This went on and on.

My mother had no idea because I was hiding this pain from her. I couldn't let her know that she was allowing me to sleep with the enemy. After all, look at what he introduced me to—and I began to like it. I thought I loved him so much, I wasn't going anywhere, so I stayed and endured the beatings, the abuse, and the drugs until, finally, one day Scott went off the deep end.

Scott drove me up to the woods on the south side of Bethlehem. There had been some killings there, but I really didn't think anything of it. He simply said, "We are just taking a ride," and I trusted him. But as we drove, an immense feeling of fear came over me. He wouldn't talk to me in the car. He just stayed quiet, like he was planning something in his head. Sure enough, after we arrived in a secluded area, Scott immediately jumped out of the car. I don't even remember there being time for him to put the car into park. He snatched me out of the car by my hair, and then in a psychotic, almost demonic rage, he began to savagely beat me, as if I were a stranger who had done something wrong to him. Punch after punch, kick after kick, he yelled and cursed at me. I was thinking to myself, "Oh no, this man is going to kill me." I screamed at the top of my lungs, until there was no more sound coming out. I'm not sure if it was the physical pain or the emotional pain that was the worst.

Scott, the love of my life, was getting ready to take my life, and no one knew where I was. As he continued to beat me, I managed to scream out, "I love you! Why are you hurting me? I love you." Then out of nowhere came a park ranger. I was so relieved, and, honestly, I think Scott was too. He had seriously lost it and didn't even know how far he had gone. I could see him come back to his senses. The ranger asked if I was OK, and I told him I was and that we were just having a minor argument. Even after all of this, I still loved him so much. The ranger allowed us to leave. In the car Scott pleaded and begged me not to leave him or tell anyone about the abuse. He desperately expressed how sorry he was and how he would never do it again. I do believe that if it weren't for the grace of God, Scott would have taken my life that day up in those woods. God sent help. I believe that ranger was my angel.

When we got back to my mother's house, the look on my mother's face showed concern and worry. She asked what had happened, and because I was afraid of Scott getting into trouble, I lied. With a smile, I said, "Yes, Mom. I'm fine. Scott and I were wrestling around, and I hit my face on the corner of the coffee table." I knew she didn't believe me, but what could she do? I chose this life with Scott, and no matter what she might have tried, I still would have been with him, because I thought I was in love and there would never be a man to love me the way Scott loved me. So, because I didn't hear her, I felt the pain as a consequence of my disobedience and rebellion. I made so many excuses for Scott and lied for him on many occasions.

After that, things simmered down a bit. There were no more fights for a while, and things were fine. Then one day Scott came over, and we were watching television in the living room. My mother didn't allow anybody anywhere else in the house (Mom wasn't having that; she demanded respect). It was getting late, and Scott didn't have a way home, so, shockingly, Mom took pity on Scott and let him sleep in the living room until the next morning when he could catch the bus home. So he stayed, but he still wasn't allowed upstairs. The next morning Mom got up and went to work. After she left, I snuck Scott upstairs to my room, and he stayed with me the whole day and left just minutes before Mom got home from work. But she found out that I had let him come upstairs, we argued and she slapped me a few times causing my nose to bleed. I saw how disappointed she was of me, but I also saw some of her own regrets. I could see that she blamed herself a little for some of the choices we were making. The sad part is that I just wouldn't listen. My mother loved me and all she wanted to do was to protect me. She had no idea what was really going on, if she had known, she would have ended the relationship for good. In hindsight, I wish I would have talked to my mother and trusted her advice and wisdom.

Once again, I believed things were going good with Scott; then I found out by one of his friends that he was cheating on me with a girl who lived across the street from his house. So I began to question things. Looking back, there was a time that he told me he sat on a stranger's toilet using the bathroom and caught crabs. So I had to shave all the hair off my body and wash all the sheets at his house in hot water. He even went so far as to buy the lotion that took away crabs and lice. He was lying about the toilet, of course, to hide his cheating. But I didn't know then; I was so young and naïve.

I truly went through some things with Scott. There were several times he made me go with him to get an HIV test. Each time after I went back for the results and found out I was negative, that's when he would go but never before me. There were so many signs I ignored.

Even after all I endured with him; I was in denial about a lot of things. I went from having this amazingly high self-esteem to a feeling of worthlessness and depression, and this went on for quite a while. Scott and I even tried to have a baby. He said it would be good for our relationship, so we tried. I wanted what he wanted, and no one was going to change that. All I wanted was Scott; but I just couldn't shake the thought of him sleeping with another female, so I decided to get even.

I stayed home more, and I began to pull away from Scott and hang out with my sisters and a few other girls from our neighborhood. Then, with perfect timing, came two guys named Carlos and Victor. Carlos wanted us to call him Thunder. I thought Thunder was cute. He was always well dressed, and the two of them had their own style. After all, they were from the Bronx, so just being different made them both attractive.

When I would go to the Penn Supreme, the neighborhood convenience store, for snacks, I would always see them. I often wondered if

Thunder had a girlfriend, but I never saw him with any girls. The only way I was going to satisfy my curiosity was to just come right out and ask him if he had a girlfriend. So I asked Thunder, and to my surprise he said he didn't have anybody; so he and I began to chat, and we started to hang out. At times when I was questioned about Scott, I would respond by saying, "Scott who?" I thought I could use the relationship with Thunder to get over Scott.

Thunder was much shorter than I was. He was very fair-skinned with the prettiest light blue eyes, like the color of an ocean. I was hooked on appearance alone. It was not that I wanted a short guy, but I figured his eyes made up for his height.

Some time went by with no Scott, but then he popped up. I initially told my sisters to tell him I wasn't there, but I was tired of lying, so I told him about Thunder and that I really liked him. Like a puppy dog Scott cried and begged for a while; but I thought to myself that I had been through enough with Scott and we needed to be apart. So I broke it off.

Shortly afterward, I practically ran to find Thunder and tell him. He knew about Scott and said when I was ready to break it off with Scott he and I could be together. So I did exactly that.

It seemed as if Thunder and I were together for a long time, but in reality it only lasted a couple of months. He was on the streets more than he was with me. I soon came to find out that he had been using heroin on a regular basis. It seemed like everyone in our community was using some kind of drugs. It was so easy to get caught up in that lifestyle. I would say to Thunder, "What's wrong with you?" because he had been acting strange, scratching and nodding. I kept getting the same answer, "Oh, nothing. I'm just tired." I knew what that meant. He wasn't just tired he was always high. I began to wonder if I was better off with Scott? At least I knew him. The fact is, neither of them was right for me. I should have left them both alone, returned home to my family, and get back to living. With all of my hidden insecurities and so much history with Scott, I found myself bouncing around between two unhealthy relationships. I just didn't want to be alone, and as the days went by, Thunder's true colors were revealed and I didn't want to start over in a new potentially abusive and destructive relationship. The heroin use also made him less attractive and my heart still ached for

Scott. As I struggled to make a final decision, I just strung them both along. I soon found out, after a few months of playing this game, and at sixteen years old, I was pregnant.

CHAPTER 5

Decisions

In any moment of decision, the best thing you can do is the right thing, the next best thing is the wrong thing, and the worst thing you can do is nothing. - Theodore Roosevelt

When I told Scott I was pregnant, he was a mixture of emotions — happy, nervous, and scared just like me. The pregnancy made him clean up his behavior and we were getting along again, but I was confused. I just didn't know what I wanted anymore. Being pregnant was a huge wake up call. I couldn't ignore what had gone on in the past, and I had to make some decisions about my future and my baby's future. The number one thing that was constantly on my mind was that I wasn't sure who the father of my child was.

Scott began to treat me like a queen. He even cooked for me. But I wasn't sure how long that would last. My faith in him being a clean, sober, faithful husband and father was shattered by what I observed and had been through during my time with him. I knew it was only a matter of time before our relationship ended for good.

When it came to telling my mom, however, I was afraid. I was afraid of letting her down and disappointing her, but I had to tell her, because soon it would be obvious. One day after school, and after hours of trying to figure out what I was going to say, I walked up the steps and in the door. I didn't know what to expect. Mom was sitting on the couch in the living room, and immediately she sensed something was troubling me, and she asked me what was wrong.

I said to her, "Mom, I have something to tell you. Please don't be upset with me. I just left Planned Parenthood. I felt I needed a checkup, and the counselor and I spoke after our conference. She asked if I wanted a pregnancy test. I said yes, and sure enough, Mom, the test was positive. I'm pregnant." She was stunned, and it took a while before she responded, but she didn't strike out in panic and anger as I assumed she would. In fact, she was very comforting and assured me that things were going to be just fine and that I had made a mistake. She said that she would help me in anyway she could, but she also said I was going to have to take care of the baby and finish school.

My mom did lecture me, but I was happy and relieved to get it. She asked me who's baby it was, and I said Scott's because I assumed that I didn't stay with Thunder long enough to get pregnant by him. She said, "Okay, let's just take things one day at a time."

So things were calm for a while. I was still in school, trying not to miss classes. I was in tenth grade with a belly, but Scott was there for me. He would take long walks with me. We cuddled, and he made me feel really good and appreciated. For a while I even believed that he finally cleaned up his act and would be the man I dreamed he could be. There was no more drug activity, and for a while, things were great.

When the time came for me to have the baby, I was living with my family. Scott and I began arguing again and I decided to go back with Thunder, even though I didn't know where he was. I couldn't imagine the idea of being alone. I had to be in a relationship even if it was the wrong one. However, I was growing weary of going back and forth and I just wanted to be with one guy in a stable relationship.

My mom and my sister Liana took me to the hospital. The contractions were coming but were not very intense, so they admitted me and put a monitor on my stomach. I was hearing the baby's heartbeat, and everything seemed to be going well. I was two weeks overdo, and people had been telling me to run around the block and do jumping jacks, and like an idiot I did. I was so tired of being pregnant and really wanted to have the baby.

For a minute after the doctors and nurses had all left, Liana was sitting on my left side, just watching things. She looked at the monitor and said something didn't seem right. I ignored it. I had never gone through something like that and didn't know what to expect. Soon a doctor came in and said, "OK, we are going to break your water." Now Liana was still on alert, and when the doctor put the instrument she used to break my water on the inside and then began to pull it out, green stuff began to squirt out. All I could see was the frown on Liana's face and the look of disgust and curiosity, as if to say, "What is this?" I knew that something wasn't right.

Liana was quite right, because shortly thereafter a team of doctors swarmed in and started working fast. I was getting scared because I heard them say they had to get the operating room ready; it was going to be an emergency. The doctors began to question me as they rolled me down the hall. It felt like the hallways were so long, and the questions were coming: When was the last time you ate? What was the last thing you ate? I was really scared because they were prepping me for an operation. Later I learned that my baby boy had passed his bowels inside of me, which poisoned my system. The umbilical cord was also wrapped around his neck. My baby was dying on the inside of me, and Liana saw that the numbers were fluctuating and it didn't seem right to her. Because he was being strangled by the umbilical cord, he passed his bowels, creating a very dangerous situation for both my baby and me.

Praise God, I woke up with a bouncing, healthy baby boy I named Laquan. But then I had to give my baby a last name. I didn't know what to do, I gave him Thunder's last name. I'm still asking myself why I did that. I didn't even know how to spell Thunder's last name. That was how little I knew about him. There I was, seventeen years old with a baby, and I didn't know where Thunder was and wasn't sure I wanted to be back with Scott. I had been with Scott for about two and a half years. There was time invested, but I was still confused about what I wanted to do.

School was not going well. I was in the tenth grade and while I was pregnant I missed a lot of days from school. When I was in school, I wasn't the nicest person to be around. I didn't like the teachers or anyone else telling me what to do. I talked back, and as a result of my unruly behavior, I had to attend alternative classes. These were classes after school from 3:00 to 5:00 p.m. That was my only option as opposed to being permanently expelled from school. I would dress my son up, and we went to class. That worked out for a while but not too long. It got to be too much, I dropped out.

Laquan was the cutest little baby I had ever seen and not just because he was mine. He was really cute, and my mom took to him quickly. And one day she just decided she was taking him permanently, and there was nothing I could do about it. She made sure of that and even said if I tried to take him she would call the police on me. She grew to love Laquan like she loved us—perhaps even more. That was fine for me because she allowed me to be a teenager. I began to hang out a bit more. I felt like luckiest girl alive. I just had a baby and my mom was willing to take care of him until I could. Although things weren't that easy, Mom became very attached and considered him to be hers, not mine; and she had every right because I still wanted to be a teen, and wasn't mature enough to raise a child.

Scott came back into the picture, and sure enough things got worse. He started to beat me regularly and the drinking and drug use became uncontrollable. I was no longer pregnant, I was using drugs with him. My life was spinning out of control. I was always on the street, hanging out. I began to realize that Scott was the worst thing that ever happened to me. Even after I convinced him that Laquan was his and he accepted that for a time, he treated me very badly. He became very controlling, and I practically lived with him, while my mom had my baby boy. Scott controlled my every step and move. I became very resentful and I was tired of living like that.

One night I happened to be just lying down listening to music, and Scott came in drunk. I knew that look in his eyes; he wanted to beat me up for nothing. I had gone through it time and time before, but that time I had enough. Scott told me to get up out of his bed and come to him. I did, and he slapped me very hard. I became enraged and hit him back, and we began to fight. In the midst of it, he said, "That's what I was waiting for this whole time: for you to fight back." I was thinking, "OK, now I know you are crazy."

That was it. I went back home and again started hanging out with my sister Liana and some girls from the neighborhood. We were hanging out in Allentown, and the whole time I was looking for a way to get away from Scott. I was afraid because he was taking things to another level and actually liked for me to fight him back.

We ran into some Jamaicans in Allentown. Winston, Rob, and Dean all lived on Broad Street by the Great Savings Groceries, in a big five-bedroom house that they split up into rooms for rent amongst family members but all males. It was fun hanging out over there. I first got familiar with Rob. It was nothing too serious to start. I thought he was cute at the time. When I met him, he was working on his car, although, anyone other than Scott was fine. I had been through enough with Scott, and I was looking for change. I hadn't completely broken it off with Scott, though, because I did love him and I didn't know where things were going to go with Rob. Every now and then I would get away and go over to the Jamaicans' house.

It was a change of scenery for the girls and me.

One time a white girl named Susan, who liked Winston, was there, along with her sister, and me and my sisters Liana and Buffy. It was so much fun, and everybody wanted to be hooked up with somebody on that particular occasion. Winston's baby's mother Marie also was there from New York. While we were all hanging out in the house, Winston had me hook him up with Susan, and he ended up having sex with her downstairs in the basement while his baby's mother was upstairs, lying in the bed and waiting for him to come. I'll tell you, back then we never really thought about certain things while they were happening. We were all living fast at such young ages, and Winston had all these guys who would come over to hang out.

I began to see more and more of Rob, and we began a sexual relationship. However, it didn't last long. He was fresh from Jamaica, and I was still dealing with Scott; and Rob didn't really want any part of it. I couldn't completely leave Scott. I knew how crazy he could get. But after calling it quits with Rob, I still hung out over there a lot. It was always fun, and we were young and still in a rebellious state of mind. We were hanging around all these guys, and it was interesting. Winston actually owned the house and was the landlord basically. He had the front room. Rob had the room in the middle, which was very tiny, just big enough to fit a queen-sized bed in there. Farther back was the bathroom, and beside that was another room. There were two more rooms up in the attic, which he rented to his brother John and his lady, who was an older Caucasian woman.

The more we hung out over there, the better Winston started to look to me. He drove many different cars. He had a red Kawasaki ninja bike. It was beautiful, and one day he asked me if I wanted a ride. I said yes, and that is where it all started. Winston was independent and always had a hustle. He was in his late twenties; kind of short—much shorter than I was—and had a stocky build to him. His money is what made him a much more attractive man, and he began to spend a lot of it on me. He bought me clothes, got my hair and nails done often. It was great to have a man spend money on me. I never had a man do for me what Winston was doing, and sex with him wasn't bad either. I began a relationship with Winston rather quickly. I was taken by his mannerisms and charm, and he treated me like a lady. He had no idea of the relationship I was trying to escape from with Scott. Rob got wind of our relationship, and I thought it would start some trouble, but I didn't care because Winston made me feel safe, as if no one could ever hurt me again. To my shock and amazement, though, Rob didn't say a word about it. After all, it was Winston's house, what could he say?

Soon after that, Scott tracked me down. Scott's best friend lived right next door to Winston, and it wasn't long before Scott knew where I was, and he found out I was over there with Winston. Scott came and demanded to see me, so I came out of the house and talked to Scott. I could see the rage in his eyes, and I was afraid. But Winston had a thing about him that made me believe he wasn't afraid of anything or anybody, and I will tell you back then Winston was ten feet tall to me even though he was about 5'8". In the back of my mind, I knew Winston wouldn't let anything happen to me. After all, I was Winston's girl now, and finally I was with someone I knew wouldn't be intimidated by Scott.

I walked out of the house and said to Scott, "What do you want?" And before he could boost himself up to fight me, I said to him, "I don't want to be with you anymore." I had had enough, and I just told him everything that was pinned up in me out of fear. Scott was the type of man who would fight me and beat me up before even trying to find out the truth; he reacted first and then wanted the truth afterwards. He had really messed me up mentally, emotionally, physically, and verbally with all kinds of bad names and language I wouldn't even repeat. Now that was my opportunity to let him have it, and I blew up on him. I told him he had made me do drugs and had found lame excuses to beat me up. He had torn down my self-esteem for the last time; it was time for me to take my life back. I was so tired of being hurt and so tired of feeling worthless, like I was in a prison because of his insecurities. Every time I left by myself and came back to him, it was always a fight. That time it was really over.

He tried to talk nice and wanted me to go back to his house. I said, "What? Do I look stupid or something? You don't have that control over me anymore. I am not afraid of you anymore." Actually, I was still afraid of him, but I couldn't show him that; he would have just used that to wheel me back in. No, not this time! I was done and not turning back. When he realized I wasn't going with him, I could see that crazed look in his eyes and I knew what was coming next; but to my amazement he looked over my shoulder and saw Winston, and it was like he curled up like a little innocent boy who could do no harm. He was scared, and that made me feel great because finally there was someone who stood up for me and defended me against a cowardice monster. I don't even think Winston really knew just how helpful it was for him to be there at that specific time. Scott got mad and said, "OK." That's all he could do. He was afraid, and he walked away, saying he didn't need me.

It was really over and I couldn't believe it! I could really move on and have a normal relationship. I walked back toward Winston, smiling. Winston was cleaning his bike and said to me, "Are you Okay?" I said yes, and he then told me to go inside and get something to drink. He had no idea how happy I was to be free. I went inside, and just a few minutes later, guess who was back? Scott! I was thinking he had worked up the nerve to beat me up in front of Winston or something, but that wasn't it. Scott came to get his gold ring that I used to wear, which had the initial J on it. I bent it really good and gave it to Winston to give to him, and that was the last time I was that close to Scott again.

I had begun a new chapter in my life. Yes, it was with another man, but the huge relief I felt being free from the abusive relationship that I knew was going no where, was worth it. The rest of it I would have to figure out later. I just knew I was happy. To think that I was with someone who couldn't even keep a job and didn't even have two dollars for gas, but had the nerve to beat me to a pulp and I put up with it.

Love doesn't hurt! No man has the right to put his hands on his spouse or any other woman in violence. Nor does a woman have the right to abuse her spouse or boyfriend. The violence in relationships must stop. There is a better way. People are not punching bags or something other people can take out their frustrations on. We are human beings, and we deserve to be loved, not controlled.

It's hard to admit that your relationship is not perfect. But no matter how you try to make it look in front of people, what is in the dark will always come to light. Sadly, by the time it surfaces, it's usually very difficult or impossible to fix. Many people lose themselves or even their lives in the process.

I should have left the first time he beat me, but I chose to stay.

I thought he loved me and that we were perfect for each other. I wanted to believe the beatings would stop and that he meant it every time he said he was sorry, but the truth is I should have left after the first violent attack. Instead, I made excuses to stay. If you are in an abusive relationship, please learn from my mistakes. You can never change a person, they have to first want it for themselves, and then be willing to make the sacrifices and changes necessary to be better. Always remember actions speak louder than words.

CHAPTER 6

The Old Manipulator

People trust their eyes above all else - but most people see what they wish to see, or what they believe they should see; not what is really there - Zoë Marriott

My life changed dramatically, and I was in a relationship with Winston. Sometimes the absence of a father or father figure will cause a woman to seek the security of an older man. My father was not stable or consistent in our lives. We didn't really have the relationship of a father and daughter and it wasn't until I got older that I grew to know him. Being with an older man I was exposed to a variety of new things; things I shouldn't have been exposed to until I became a woman. I was seventeen years old with a baby, and Winston was a twenty-nine years old man that I didn't know very much about. It didn't matter to me that the details of his life were a bit blurry, because I was free. There was no more abuse just good times; things were great, life was getting better and I could finally relax. I traveled with Winston everywhere he went. I was really falling for him because he made me feel special, wanted and appreciated; he made me feel like I was a queen. Winston gave me things, took me clothes shopping, got my nails done, and gave me money. I was so taken with Winston and impressed with the lavish lifestyle that he was showering me with, I wasn't willing to give him up. I thought I had a prize, a man who was good for me and accepted me for who I was. At nights when we slept, he would hold me in his arms. In the daytime around other people, Winston never really displayed that sensitive side. He was a bad boy and others looked up to him, and some even feared him, but I liked that image also. However, nights were my favorite times with Winston, he was warm and welcoming in private. Because of that, I would sleep like a baby safe and secure; and we slept as if there was nothing else in the world but the two of us at that moment. My fear, anxiety, and nervousness slowly melted away in his arms. Winston was everything I wanted in a man, a real man, a man with an income, a man who could take care of me, a man with whom I felt safe.

Being around Winston made me believe that I had hope for a better future, and the idea of being a mother was something I started to embrace. I wanted to get closer to my baby, because I knew I was in a healthier environment. I knew that trying to take him away from my mother was another story. On one day in particular, I had him with me over at Winston's house and he spent the night with us. The next morning, my mother was outside honking the horn and banging on the door like there was a fire. She wanted my son Laquan, whom she had grown so attached to. That was the first time I witnessed the hatred my mother felt for Winston. She knew he was too old for me, and she used to call him "old manipulator". She believed that he manipulated me with his money, cars, and houses. And, honestly, he did use those things to entice me, but I wanted them. He was willing to give me the things I wanted, and I was not passing them up, not after what I went through in my previous relationships. I wanted to be Winston's girl, and for the first time I began to feel as if I deserved it all.

My mother never cursed, but that day she let Winston have it. I was shocked and surprised, but what was most shocking was his response; he cursed right back at her. It reaffirmed that I was dealing with a man with pride and not a little boy. To quiet the situation, I handed over my son to my mother. At that time he was about six months old. I stayed several more days at Winston's house. Then when I thought mom had cooled down, I went back home. There was still so much tension at home, but after a few days, things simmered down and were OK again.

Being with Winston allowed me to be young and free, and I enjoyed that feeling, but it never lasted long. I was always aware that I was a mother and my son was not with me. I would always come back to that reality and inner turmoil, and it would fill me with guilt and remorse. I was living my life while someone else was raising my child. Ironically, that same reality was what allowed me to fall so deep into my folly. I was still going back and forth between houses, and in a similar way I was torn between my love for my family, and my desire to be young and free. I didn't see a way to have both.

Winston began traveling a lot to New York while I was at his place or at home with my mom. I had a key to his house and could come and go as I pleased. I began hanging out with my friends again. My very best friend at the time was Karen. Karen and her family had moved to

Bethlehem from Alabama, and she and her siblings spoke with a very deep country accent. When she arrived, we hit it off instantly because Karen was a lot like me. She was also very tall, and could relate to me in so many ways. We got along well, and before you knew it we were best friends. We got so close that at first it bothered my triplet sister Liana. I tried my best to include her in things, but I limited just how many things I would allow her to take part in because I felt I had to protect her. Even though I was only two minutes older, I still had to be her big sister and shield her from certain dangers like drugs.

When Winston traveled to New York, I stayed home a lot more, hanging out and having fun just being a teenager. I even began to feel more relaxed because I could be close to my son without worrying about Winston. Then Karen and I began to get involved in drug activity—this time it was marijuana. One of my guy friends wanted us to sell it, and we did. We enjoyed doing it too. It allowed us to make some extra money without having to do much work. Things were going fast, and they had to because I wasn't keen on taking drugs to my mom's house, no matter what it was, and Winston's house was too far for me to take the bus everyday. Eventually, Winston asked me about it, and I told him. He didn't like the idea of me selling drugs and wanted me to stop, I did for a while.

Afterwards, Winston stayed home for a long time and didn't take any trips, he and I became close again. I was not feeling well one day. I was nauseated and thought that feeling was very familiar; I laid down flat on my back and began to press on my lower abdomen. I felt a little knot. I said, "Oh no, not again." I went the next morning to the neighborhood Planned Parenthood and took a pregnancy test. Sure enough, I was pregnant again. I wasn't as afraid that time because I knew Winston would take good care of me, and he did when he was in town. He was still going back and forth, but when he knew he was leaving, he gave me money and really made me feel like he was interested in our pregnancy and me. When I told Mom, she wasn't very angry, I think she knew that it was inevitable; but she did say I was going to have to step it up and take care of my second baby. Of course, she didn't really care for Winston at all, and I expected her response.

I was still hanging out with Karen, but without my knowledge, she had begun to sell cocaine. I was no stranger to that, but I was sure that lifestyle was over with. Thank God, I was pregnant because I refused to use drugs while I was pregnant. I didn't even want to smoke cigarettes. I was happy to be pregnant by Winston, and I felt really good about it. It was also nice to be sure who the father of my baby was that time, and know that he would be able to take care of us. However, I still chose to hang out with Karen despite the fact that she was now selling cocaine.

My belly was growing and things were progressing. We hung out a lot, and Winston dropped in from time to time. I was nine months pregnant and as big as a house. I went from weighing 160 pounds to 225 pounds, and my nose started to spread way across my face. However, all of my weight was in my belly. From the back I was as flat as a board, but from the side and the front, I was like Humpty Dumpty, very big and round. I was so tired, and like most women, at nine months I just wanted to have the baby. My original due date was around February 2. I was overdue by two whole weeks. After going to my checkup, the doctor decided to induce my labor. Winston was in New York at the time, they called him, and he got on the road immediately with a couple of his friends. He actually made it in time for my delivery. However, my mother was already there, and they just couldn't be in the same room. My mother put me on the spot and gave me an ultimatum. She said boldly, "If he is staying, I am leaving." There was no way I was going to choose a man over my mother. Even though that would have been my first experience with a man who actually wanted to be a part of the delivery and our lives, my mother had spoken, and what she said was law. Winston drove down from New York and had to sit in the waiting room. Although my mother and I did have our differences, she took precedence in my life at that time. When no one was there for me, Mom was. Even though she didn't want me with the "old manipulator," she was always there, over and over again.

As hours went by I pushed when they said to push however I was having a very hard time because my baby didn't want to come out. I was in labor for something like two days, and finally with the assistance of the forceps and suction, our son was born. He weighed nine pounds, twelve ounces. Winston was there for me, and I thought it was the least I could do. Our son came out looking like he was a three-month-old baby. He wasn't hard to spot in the nursery because he was the biggest baby there. He was so cute. He came out as light as tan, but his ears were dark, so we were there trying to figure out what complexion he was going to have.

After our baby was born and his dad got to look at him, he left to get some sleep. Meanwhile, Mom wasn't budging. She was always there. When the time came for us to leave, to my shock and amazement my mother did let Winston pick up the baby and I from the hospital and take us back to her house. Things were calm for a while. Months went by with Winston popping in every now and then, dropping off things for our baby and money. My mother saw how he was trying to be a good father, she eased off of him a bit; but shortly thereafter things began to flare up again.

At the time, I was there with my two babies, along with my sisters and their babies. Mom still tried to help everyone. I had two sons there, my triplet sister Liana had given birth to a set of twins and my sister Buffy had given birth to her first son as well. All the babies were around the same age, with the exception of my son Laquan who was born first and was two years old at the time. Not to mention, my brother hadn't yet left the house either and my mother also allowed my dad to come in from time to time, truly she displayed unconditional love toward us all and put up with a lot. It made perfect sense that her mood would change from time to time. Our mother had the weight of the world on her shoulders with no one to ease her load or take any of the weight. She had to be strong for everyone.

In all of that I never really heard our mother complain nor did she ever make any of us feel like we were not wanted there; in fact, she welcomed all of us with her love, actions, attention and support. She shopped for the entire house and cooked for everybody when she wasn't at work. I actually enjoyed cleaning when she would ask me to. I would do the best job I could because the happiness and joy she displayed afterwards was most rewarding.

The house however, was getting entirely too small for six young babies, and six adults. My sister Buffy came up with the bright idea of getting an apartment not too far from our mother's house. The apartment was only five minutes from our mother's house in walking distance. It was a one-bedroom apartment, and it seemed like a good idea at the time. In fact, it was the best thing I had heard in a long time. And if she was leaving, so was I. I liked the idea of having my own place with no one telling me what to do or when to do it. I got used to living away from home periodically, but for Buffy that was a major decision because Buffy had always stayed close to our mother. Our mother was really protective of her. Buffy was very obedient and a good girl; when she became pregnant, it did hurt our mother, but we were growing up and making a lot of our own decisions, even though they weren't always the best decisions.

After seeing things going well for Buffy, I asked Buffy if I could move in and help her, and she said yes. I packed up our things, and my baby and I were gone. That was going to be my first experience totally out of the house. I was looking forward to Winston coming down to visit, and I felt good about him actually being able to come in and sit with me. My sister Buffy had the bedroom, while I had the living room. In my teenage mind, it was a great setup! It was ours, and there was no one to tell us what to do.

My sister's boyfriend and his friend would come down from Philly and stay for a couple of days with us. We decided since we paid our own bills and were now responsible for our own lives that we could also drink if we wanted to. My sister Buffy kept the fridge filled with food and cleaned continuously; it was a very peaceful atmosphere. She was a great roommate and an awesome sister. I never had any issues with my sister Buffy. She never judged me or hurt me in any way. In fact, right after she dropped out of school, she began working at the factory with my mother, Buffy worked there for 22 long years, I applaud her for that. That showed dedication and endurance. When we were living at home Buffy used to pay me faithfully $50 weekly to watch her son, my nephew Stephon, and her $50 was guaranteed. When Friday came Buffy came in from work and would just hand me the money like clockwork. She never gave anyone any reason to talk about her. Buffy always paid her way. My mother did have a major impact on her. Buffy proved to be a great friend as well as a great sister.

Winston was out of town constantly, and I was feeling a bit lonely. In fact, I had started to question why Winston was always gone, and I allowed my mind to believe that something was going on with Winston and another woman. I didn't have any hard evidence or proof, all I could do was assume. It happened that Buffy's boyfriend came down to visit with his friend Chris, and the four of us were hanging out. I was starting to become attracted to Chris. He was always flirting with me, and I started to flirt back. Our mom was babysitting for us, it was just Buffy and I, along with our guests and a few drinks, and that spelled trouble. I knew better, because I was always faithful to Winston. I think it was Chris's blue eyes and suave style that did it. He and I began to talk, and the talking then led to kissing, and the kissing led to touching. Before I knew it, we were lying down on the living room floor in heated passion, and then it happened. I had cheated. I didn't feel as bad because in my mind I had convinced myself that Winston was cheating; I made myself believe that it was right when it was wrong.

Afterwards we were there chilling, and to my shock and amazement, who comes knocking at the door? Winston! And Chris was in there with me! I was panicked, but I opened the door. There was some tension, but I managed to calm the situation down. Winston and I went outside and talked. I know he knew something had happened, but I wasn't going to be stupid enough to volunteer any information either. I went back with Winston to his house. We talked, I showered, and we went to bed and woke up fresh like nothing ever happened. By the time we got back over to the apartment, Chris had left, and I was glad for that. I went back to my mom's and picked the kids up.

We were in the apartment about three months, and sadly things started to get tight financially. First, the cable got turned off and then the gas. Buffy and I agreed that things weren't going too well and that we might have to go back home. Because Winston was back and forth so often, it didn't make sense to be in Allentown with our son when he was gone, and it was getting cold—way too cold for babies—my sister and I decided we had to go back, and our mother knew it. From the day we came up with the idea, our mother knew we were going to have to experience it because we weren't taking no for an answer. We were of age and thought we were capable of supporting ourselves and living on our own. Yes, we were wrong, but we had to see that for ourselves, and we did. We humbly went back home, thank God our mother graciously accepted us. Thank God for our mother. She was always our mother, always parenting. Even in her silence she taught us that we needed to listen or we would suffer, and suffer we did.

We were all back home, and it was a tight fit, we managed. I went back to babysitting for Buffy, and that $50 began to come in again, along with the money I was getting from Winston every now and then. Things were financially difficult for everyone, and I began to see less of Winston and started hanging out with Karen again, even though she was still selling. I have come to learn that if you hang around someone long enough you start to do some of the same things they do and that was exactly what happened to me. I began selling again. Then Winston started to question me. He asked me if I was selling, and I said, "Yes, I have to do something to get more money." Instead of him giving me more money to prevent me from selling drugs, he began to give me drugs to sell for him. I did that for a while. I was young, and I thought I was discreet, but my sister Liana began to ask questions, I told her what I was doing. Often she asked if she could hang out with me, often times I would say no. I didn't want her to have anything to do with it. I knew what drugs were; my sister Liana didn't, and I wanted it to stay that way.

Karen and I were hanging out all the time now, and I was paying my mom to babysit. One of our customers was a girl named Mary. Mary would buy from us often. When she came it was late and her face was always sweaty and her eyes were very wide. At the time I was saying to myself, "Wow, she looks bad." And I began to think, "I will never end up like that." I was judging her without even knowing it, but I would look at her like I was better than she was because I was the dealer, not the crack addict. I thought of myself as better than she was, but in actuality I was no better; in fact, I was just as bad, if not worse, because I saw and knew firsthand what these drugs did to people, and yet I still chose to sell that poison to people.

Karen decided to move out of her mom's house, and guess who she went to live with? The drug addicted girl who was buying crack from us, Mary. Karen would just give her drugs to stay there, which was fine with Mary. Winston had a stash over at his house, and he couldn't come down from New York, and he told me where the drugs were in the house. There were ten eight balls, one eight ball could bring anywhere from $80 to $100, and if you broke it down and bagged it up into twenties, you could get anywhere from $120 to $160 depending on how much you stepped on it (added cut to stretch it). I was too scared to take that many eight balls back to my mother's house, I asked Karen to keep them for me there at Mary's house. That was a bad idea because both of them used drugs at the time, and Karen and I had been putting cooked-up cocaine into weed and smoking it. Karen told me she would hold on to them for me. I left them there and went home. I was uneasy about the whole thing, but there was nothing else I could do. I was not going to jeopardize my mom's house. That just wasn't going to happen.

The next day I was sitting in the bathtub when I remembered the drugs at Mary's house. I hurried through my bath and headed out the door. It was a sunny day without a cloud in the sky. Things seemed perfect, maybe too perfect. I got to Mary's front door and knocked and knocked. I had brought my sister with me because I had a bad feeling despite the sun shining and the day looking great. When no one would come to the door, I became very impatient. I knocked and called and got no response; I became even angrier and I kicked the door in. Sure enough there was Mary, eyes wide open like she had been smoking all night. Karen was in the bathroom washing her face. I asked Karen where my stuff was and immediately she acted like she was going for the stash. She came back with three eight balls and said Mary must have searched the house, found the stash, and smoked them up. I turned to Mary and said, "Where's my stuff?" She couldn't even talk. It was like her mouth was glued shut. Her hair was all over the place, and she was sweating like she was in the shower with her clothes on. She just stood there looking at me with her eyes wide open, like they were being held that way.

I just blanked out. I lost all patience and control. I began to beat her like she was my worst enemy, and as far as I was concerned, she was. After all, they weren't my drugs; they belonged to my kid's father, and he was already suspecting me of using. That was just going to make things worse. I went crazy, trashing her place. I picked up her stereo and said to her, "So you want to smoke up my drugs? Okay, so how much is this stereo worth?" She was still very high that she couldn't talk. I threw the stereo at her and began to whale on her and beat her. To be honest she was so high I doubt she even felt it. In fact, she might have had some of the drugs left over and just decided it was worth the beating to hold on to them while I took what I already had. So, out of ten balls, all I had were three balls left.

After we all beat Mary, including Karen who helped her smoke the drugs, I was good and tired. I called Winston and told him what had happened. He was furious. I was scared, but I did tell him the truth. After that, things started to get bad. Winston refused to take anything less than full payment. He made sure of it. He started giving me drugs and stressed that he wanted every dime from them. I then started taking mine off the top and what he asked for I gave to him. I made sure that when he came I gave him every dime. He even made me sit at his kitchen table after I was done selling the drugs because the money wasn't organized. He said it was too messy, he made me sit and organize every bill that was there—the ones with the ones, the fives with the fives, the tens with the tens, and the twenties with the twenties. Things were really bad, and I felt I was just being used to make money for him as opposed to being his baby's mother, the one he loved and catered to once upon a time.

Winston could sense things were going wrong, and he was right. I was starting to use a lot more, and that worried him. I could tell because we talked and he informed me of the fact that he had to get rid of the house on Broad Street. He decided to move our baby and me into an apartment down the alley from my mom's house; I thought that was a great idea. It did slow me down, although I didn't completely stop messing around with drugs. The friendship between Karen and I had deteriorated and eventually ended completely.

Winston was still back and forth to New York, but he had put me into an apartment, I was safe. It was a small attic apartment on the third floor, with one bedroom, a living room, a small dining area, and a tiny kitchen. It was just enough for us. I felt like I was getting back the Winston I had fallen for in the very beginning. So much had happened since the time we met, and I was ready for things to calm down. I wanted him to love and appreciate me again, as he had before. I wanted to be more than a sometimes sex partner. I wanted to be his, I wanted to fix the mess I created I just didn't know what to do but what I did know is that I wanted for him to be mine again.

CHAPTER 7

What's Done in the Dark

For nothing is secret, that shall not be made manifest; neither any thing hid, that shall not be known and come abroad. - Luke 8:17

I don't remember where I heard the rumor first, but there was a rumor that Winston, the love of my life, and father of my child had another family in New York. I wouldn't allow myself to believe it. I didn't want to believe it because things were just beginning to get back to normal, whatever that was. He was spending some time with our baby and me, and I was trying to play house in the small apartment he rented for us, doing the best I could. I remember making him some pork chops and rice, and even though the pork chops were very salty, he ate them to make me feel good. I was really trying, and I thought he was too; I just could not let another woman have my man. However, in order for another woman to have your man, he has to be a willing participant, and he was. I eventually confirmed that the rumor was true he really did have another family. Winston was living a double life. That explained where he would be weeks and months on end. I thought I was his woman, his only woman; and not only was I not his only woman, but I wasn't even number one.

After so much time together he got sloppy and did a bad job of hiding it, though he didn't have to because I just didn't want to know. As long as he didn't flaunt it in front of me, I was still going to be with him. I still needed him in my life and I didn't have a back up plan. I depended on Winston to pay the bills and take care of our son, which he did for a while. After some time in the small apartment, it was Winston's idea to move our baby and me to Allentown into a bigger apartment. At the time it seemed like a good idea. The rent was cheaper, and the place was bigger. The kitchen was located around the back. As you walked through, making your way from the kitchen, you came to the living room and then to the right was the bathroom, and in the very front of the apartment was the bedroom. It was still one bedroom, but it was bigger than the last apartment so that was fine. That was necessary since I found out I was pregnant with our second son. That's right, I was nineteen going on twenty, and I was pregnant with my third baby. I had become a statistic with no real plans, and making no effort to improve my life, I wasn't worried because I loved Winston and I knew he would take care of us. I still believed that we had a chance for a future. He bought some beautiful curtains for the apartment and other small things, and I appreciated it. I was willing to accept any small gesture as a sign that he still wanted to be with me.

Winston assured me things would get better and that he would always be there for us. That was partially true. I was receiving welfare assistance and collecting food stamps and WIC, so the government was taking care of us. The little of Winston that I saw I accepted because it meant that at least some part of him still cared for me and I believed that he loved me because he was still coming to see us. But at the time I was still messing with drugs.

I told myself I could stop, but as soon as Winston would leave, I would call his cousin Rob and ask him to bring me some powder to sniff. Even though I was pregnant and said I would never use drugs while I was pregnant, I was only lying to myself. Up until that point, I had never actually used drugs while I was pregnant, but I was alone with the kids, away from my family and could think of nothing better to do than to use cocaine. I still did the best I could as a mother, but really that wasn't very good. I was still using drugs while trying to pay the bills, trying to keep the house clean, and trying to keep up our baby's shots and my doctors' appointments.

I hid many things from my mom , especially the drug use because I wanted her to believe that I was responsible enough to do it on my own. And because she trusted me, she brought my son Laquan over to be with me. I was actually able to potty train my son Laquan, which was a good thing because it made me feel like I was doing something right. My mom still had him living with her, and it was too much of a fight to try to get him from her, so I allowed him to stay with her. There were no courts involved or legal procedures. She simply took him. He was just hers, and it was okay. My hands were full. I was trying, but despite my efforts I couldn't manage my life, it had spun out of control.

Despite not always being in my right mind, I was still functioning. I still went food shopping and tried desperately to appear to be sober, but when a person is using drugs frequently, it always gets worse. Things began spinning faster out of control. I started calling Rob a lot more, and for the first time in my life, even after telling myself I would never do it, I had sex for drugs. I had sex with Winston's cousin Rob. That was the same Rob I dated briefly years before when he first came from Jamaica and was renting a room from Winston. We decided to keep it between us. I think he still had feelings for me, which was convenient at the time because I didn't have the money to buy the drugs. I would just call Rob, and he delivered them to me.

Winston started hitting me every now and then, and I believed that was fine because what I was doing was wrong and I didn't know how to stop; and I accepted it. When Winston and I argued, he called me all kinds of names and smacked me around. That only made me want to use more to numb the pain and the ugliness that my life had become. I couldn't wait for him to leave so I could call Rob and feel better.

I was still pregnant, and I tried to get clean because I didn't want any drugs to show up in my baby's system. Thankfully, when I delivered my third son, he was drug free and I was twenty years old.

$$* \quad * \quad * \quad * \quad * \quad * \quad *$$

Things were calm for a while, and I was trying to be a good mom and do the best I could, but I still had that thing inside me that made me believe I needed the cocaine to function. I began to use again, only that time things got worse. I began sharing drugs with my neighbors upstairs from me, and then rent time came around. My landlord's name was Anne. Ironically, many years before when my mother moved us from the projects on the north side of Bethlehem, we moved into a building on the south side of Bethlehem. Anne and her husband owned that building as well. Shockingly, I found out that Anne used drugs too. In fact, she sniffed so much drugs, I didn't have to pay her in cash. I gave her drugs, and she would write the receipt as if I gave her rent money. That was great because I could just buy a couple of eight balls, bag it out and stretch it, and then give everything to her as if I were giving her a lot. In reality, I was only spending about $200 dollars and bagging it out and then giving it to her that way. I didn't have to give her all my money and I still had some drugs left over for me.

I was still functioning somewhat. After being up for long periods using cocaine my body demanded sleep, I would lock the apartment up tight, bathe the kids and feed them, and then I would go to sleep. After getting some sleep, I was OK again for a while. Then when my mind would take me again, I did it all over again, using the drugs. And if I didn't have the money, I would call Rob. He was the only one I was getting the drugs from at the time. Winston wasn't going to trust me again with the drugs. That was a wrap as far as he was concerned, and for good reason too. I had started using just as quickly as I got it.

The way I was paying Anne soon came to an end. I would buy the drugs, but by the time Anne got there, there wasn't much left to give her for rent; and because there wasn't enough, she threatened to evict me. I never thought she would do that because if she did, I could tell on her. One day I packed the kids up and went to my mom's. I just needed to get away and be around familiar faces. When I got back to my apartment, it was locked up. Anne had changed the locks, so I went in through a window, opened the door, and got out as much stuff as I could—my clothes, the kids' clothes, my floor-model television—and took the things upstairs to the neighbors I used to give drugs to and get high with. They kept them until I was able to get a ride and gather my things from them. While Anne thought she was hurting me, she wasn't hurting me; I was hurting me. I was beginning to spin out of control and couldn't get a grip.

I called Winston, and he told me not to worry. Sure enough, when Winston came down from New York, he helped me get into another apartment on the south side of Bethlehem across from a bar named Carlito's Bar and Grille and a graveyard, which I was afraid of. But I didn't have a choice; I had to live there. The apartment itself was great. It was like a townhouse. It was the nicest place I ever had up to that point. It was a three-bedroom house, big and spacious, and nowhere near any projects. It was definitely better living. There was an upstairs and a downstairs. As you walked into the house, there were steps leading upstairs, and to the right was a big, spacious living room. A bit farther back was a dining room area, and to the left prior to entering the kitchen was another small room that was big enough for a sofa bed and TV. The kitchen was at the back of the house. Even though he didn't like the woman I had become as a cocaine user, Winston still did things for us. I thought things were going to get better for us, but it was just the opposite. Winston stayed for a little while with me. I felt safe, and I wasn't using. I was taking care of our children, and getting along great with my family.

Sometime after we were all moved in, Winston came up with another story, saying he had to leave to take care of some business. I was in my own place alone with my children, left to make my own decisions again. My mind began to wander, and like a predictable pattern it happened: I called Rob. I had money, the house was filled with food, the kids were OK, and the house was clean. I was thinking I had done everything I had to do; now I could get high—and I did. And all the while, no one knew but Rob and me. There were times I had money and times I didn't. I was collecting welfare, so I had an income. I was about twenty-one years old with two of my three sons.

Every time money came into my hands, my next move was to call and get some cocaine; and that was almost daily. I will never forget the feeling my body started to go through as I waited for the drugs to arrive. I felt nauseated, as if I were getting ready to vomit. My hands would get clammy. I felt like I had to go take a dump. Oh, my goodness, I was so tired of that feeling, but I put myself through that, because I just couldn't stop. I thought I was functioning. The bills were paid, the house was clean, there was food in the cabinets, and the kids were stable. I was thinking everything was fine; I had it all under control. But I didn't have it under control.

When Rob stopped coming as often, I had to find other ways to get the cocaine. I began to hang out across the street at the bar. It was a Hispanic bar, but it didn't matter because there were drugs everywhere. It seemed like every Hispanic person I met either sold cocaine or used it. In reality, I only dealt with certain types of people, and therefore my views of people were very limited. The bar became my second home. It was not normal behavior, but I couldn't see it because I was so bound up by the drugs. It was getting so bad that if I didn't have the cocaine, I was a very mean person. I became very moody and anxious and easily agitated. I stopped really taking care of myself; and, of course, if I wasn't able to take care of myself, I wasn't going to be able to take care of my children either, but I tried.

Things become complicated when you start to live for drugs. Winston was starting to stay away for longer periods of time, and I was getting worse. Back then when I would go to the bar across the street, I would go tell my next-door neighbor, Thomas, to keep watch on the kids for a few minutes. I would run over for an hour or so while my neighbor watched the kids. But then I began to stay too long. Thomas would say he was watching the kids, but then I would come home and the kids were all alone. I thought they were safe because I left them with a responsible adult. But really how responsible was he? He used drugs as much as I did, and he had all kinds of things going on at his house. Now I will admit on several occasions he did help me out, but I guess I began to burn those bridges. All I was able to see clearly was the cocaine and schemes to get more. I didn't even want weed anymore. It slowed me down, and it was my last option. If I couldn't get anything else, then weed it was. When I woke up after smoking the weed, I would take a look around at my kids and feel so bad. I would ask myself, why? But it didn't stop me. After I cleaned up the house and fed the kids and cleaned them up, I went right back to the same routine.

After Rob began to show up less and less, I began to call Rob's brother Richard. He had just come from Jamaica, and he didn't know much about anything, but he knew how to deliver. I called him up one day and told him I wanted a pack. He came, and this went on a few more times. Then I called him, but I didn't have any more money; I told him we could work it out another way, and we did. He got what he wanted, and so did I. From that point on, whenever I called, he came. Now it was no longer a matter of whether Rob wanted to come or not. Though he still found time to come occasionally, it didn't really matter because if he said no, his brother said yes. Rob saw the state I was in and was worried about me and really wanted me to stop. He tried to tell me to stop after a while, and that I was hurting myself, but I didn't want to hear any of that. After all, I was my own person, and everything I decided to do I could do because I paid my own bills—sometimes at least. I still couldn't see past the drugs. I was truly sick but didn't know how bad it was. I was officially addicted.

My mom would call me every now and then when my phone was on. She didn't come too often, probably because she didn't want to see me in the state I was in, and it was getting really bad. One day, though, my mom let me know she was coming up to the house. I thought, "I am going to clean up now and pull myself together. I don't want my mom to worry or see me all messed up." I cleaned up and cleaned up the kids. I showered and did my hair and my makeup, and I thought I looked good. My plan was to call for some drugs after my mom left, but when she got to the house, the look on her face when she saw me hurt me. I didn't understand what she was seeing. I thought I looked good, but I really looked bad. My mom told me to look at myself. She said my lips weren't lined right, and after she said it I went to look in the mirror, and she was right. My bottom lip was lined in velvet black eyeliner, and the line didn't meet up with my lip line. My neck was dirty—for some reason I kept missing my neck when I bathed. Clearly, things weren't right, so my mom said. "Let's go. I'm taking you to get some help."

CHAPTER 8

Addiction

The best way out is always through. ~ Robert Frost

This was the first attempt at rehabilitation. We went to the shelter on the south side of Bethlehem on Wyandotte Street. My mom didn't really know what to do, but I was her baby girl, and she tried to get help. She was scared for my life and had no idea that things were as bad as they were. We sat and talked to a counselor, and I was as honest as a cocaine addict could be. I could remember in my mind I was always contemplating and planning and trying to hustle up another dollar, and I wouldn't stop until I got what I wanted. I had become the "old manipulator". The counselor suggested to my mom that I go to detoxification and then rehab immediately. I wanted to please my mom, and I said I would go, but I got out of it quickly and went back to the same old ways. An addict has to want to be clean, and willing to at least try to commit, because detoxification is not an easy process. Part of the reason why addicts become addicted and increase usage and frequency is trying to suppress the withdrawal symptoms that detox brings on. If an addict is not at least willing to suffer through the withdrawals and other symptoms of detox they will go back to their old ways and things almost always get worse. When I got back home things got worse.

I began to smoke crack with my neighbor, Thomas, the same person I used to have watching my children. I got to a state where I made excuses for everything to seem right. I couldn't think straight. All I could see was the drugs. The cocaine was my food. Soon things began to disappear from my house, as I began selling them for drug money because things really got tight. The whole time I just couldn't see what was really going on. No matter what anyone tried to do or say, I just couldn't see it.

Soon I began to have other people hanging out at my house. People were using my bathroom to shoot up heroin, the drug I was terribly afraid of. In exchange for allowing them to use in my house, they would give me crack. That was how I stayed high. Honestly, I don't know how I took care of my kids. But what I do know is that God's grace not only covered me it covered them too. God had them. Things were so bad that when I cleaned my house, I picked up a bent needle from a syringe off the floor. People were coming at all times of the night. If you had told me that was going to be one of the results from drug use, I would have argued that it was not possible to have that kind of traffic through one's house, but I lived it.

One night Winston came down to visit. Normally when he came, he would pop in late, but this time there had been some people there using heroin shortly before he arrived. I told the people to leave when Winston popped up. I was surprised to see him because of how little he had been coming. He was not happy at the condition of the house and the kids. There was no food. I had spent up the money and food stamps on crack, and there was nothing to eat. I could see the anger in him but more than anything, the hurt in him. I loved Winston because even though he beat me and wasn't with us much, when he did come he would fix things. And even then when he lay beside me, he would still hold me in his arms. All I wanted was to be loved. However, that particular night three of the people who used to hang out at my house and shoot heroin came back to the house and knocked on the door. I answered, and they asked if they could come in. I told them no, that my kids' father was there. I did want Winston more than I wanted the drugs, but it was a constant fight back and forth. I could not control the addiction. It was like something had taken over me. In a low tone so Winston couldn't hear me, I said to Joey, the Hispanic man who was accompanied by two women, "Not tonight." Joey refused to take no for an answer. He tried to talk me into letting them use my house to have a threesome and said he was going to pay me. I said I couldn't do it. Then he showed me the crack. I thought about it, but I couldn't say yes. We needed things in the house, and if I said yes, Winston would leave. I didn't allow it that night.

One of the things I cherished was the time I spent with Winston. Whether I was using or not, he still wrapped his arms around me at night. But I still was sick in my mind, still controlled by the drugs. When he went to sleep, I found where he stashed the money and took some of it from under the mattress. He was quite calm, too calm, when he realized what I had done. Then I discovered why. He said the money I stole from him was for me. He said if I wanted the things that we needed, like toilet tissue, toothpaste, clothes detergent, deodorant, diapers, and food, I had better use the money I stole and go buy them. It was only $100, but it was enough to get what we needed. I gave it back to him, and we went to the store and got some of the things we needed for the house and the kids. Winston did try to talk to me about my behavior. I found out his first wife, did the same thing. She was messed up on crack too, so he had experienced these things before. I knew he was disappointed by what I had become, and he felt some guilt for how bad things spun out of control. When he met me I was just a teenager with a kid, and now because of him and the choices we both made, I was left to deal with immense responsibilities without his help, and he was no longer around to protect me.

Soon Winston had to leave again, and each time he left, things got worse and worse. There was a guy I didn't know very well who asked if he could use my bathroom if he paid me in crack. Reluctantly, I said yes. The boys and I went back and sat in the living room for a while. I just didn't trust that one, so after the kids were calm and distracted, I went into the kitchen and did the crack. The guy was upstairs and taking too long. After my high wore down a bit, I went up to see what was going on and to make sure that man wasn't dead up in my bathroom. He was alive, but he did a lot of heroin and couldn't get up. I told him he had to leave because I was getting ready to go. Slowly but surely he left after I started to get loud, he began to see that I was not playing games. Once I finally got him out of my house, I went back upstairs to make sure he hadn't left any drugs or syringes behind. When I got into my bathroom, what I saw made me decide that things were really getting out of control. There was blood squirted all over the walls and ceiling. It was clear it came straight from his veins because there were thin streams of blood everywhere. Immediately, I went into mother mode, which prompted defense mode. I gave the kids some snacks, and I got some bleach and a bucket and dish washing liquid and scoured that whole bathroom. Now that was crazy and too close to danger. A few of the people who came to my house were infected with AIDS I was told, but I didn't pay much attention to it because all I wanted was the drugs, and I wasn't sleeping with them. But when that blood was splattered all over my walls, I decided enough was enough.

I cleaned up and stopped allowing people to use drugs at my house for a while. I was beginning to get scared. It was almost like a slap in the face when reality set in. I pulled myself together. I didn't want any more of the using. I wanted to take care of my kids, so I spent some quality time with them. We would watch movies and eat chips in the living room while all the lights were turned off, so if people would come, they would think I was asleep or not at home. I was just done with it.

Then I started to talk to some old high school friends. I saw one of the girls I used to go to school with at the gas station. I was still not in my right mind. I had stopped the physical use but my mindset was still affected. I was sick mentally. She and I caught up and reminisced about the old days when we were attending middle school. After reminiscing about the past and where life had taken us—minus all my negatives—she introduced me to her boyfriend. He was an Asian guy. I had never really been attracted to an Asian guy before, and I never thought that it could possibly go anywhere with me being in the condition I was in. I was truly beat down by low self-esteem and drug abuse. I was just going with the flow, but I could see some attraction between us. I got his number after we were all hanging out, and I decided to call him. We set up a date without his girlfriend, my high school mate, and he came to my house. I got a sitter, and he picked me up and took me to a diner far away. I didn't think much of it really. I was a bit bothered, but I didn't think much of myself. The customers at the diner were predominantly white. There was no way I would run into anyone I knew or he knew. I think the whole point was not to run into anyone who knew him, which was fine with me. I was happy that he thought enough of me to take me out regardless of where he took me. I ordered a California cheeseburger and French fries, and he ordered the same.

I was so naïve I felt privileged that this guy wanted to take me out; when in actuality he was hiding me. That's just how things were for me at that time, though. After we were finished eating, we went back to his apartment. You know the story. I guess for that little burger and fries he felt I owed him something. So, yes, I did what I call sex by guilt. I felt since he had taken me out, I had to sleep with him. After all, I knew it would not go any farther. He had a girlfriend and I had a monkey on my back that I couldn't get rid of, besides, I felt no one would want me. I had sex with him with minimal foreplay. Things went quickly, and soon it was over. I really didn't feel the way he might have because he cheated on his girlfriend. I didn't even know if I had a relationship or not because Winston was in and out, back and forth. I just existed. After Kurt and I cleaned up a bit, he drove me home. There was no kiss, only "I'll see ya later." I was fine with that. I knew it wasn't going anywhere. I got what I could, which was a burger and fries and mercy sex.

The next day my kids' father Winston came back. I was quite uninterested in him. The longer he stayed away, the more I grew out of love with him, or so I thought. Kurt called me the next day, and Winston happened to be standing there listening. I didn't care because I wasn't stupid. When he wasn't there with me, I knew he was with another woman so I made sure to talk loud. Sure, Kurt was full of it and I knew the truth, but I played along with him. We talked about hooking up and how much fun we had. Winston was listening the whole time and asked who was on the phone. I said it was a friend of mine, and when he asked what friend, I said it was Kurt. I could see the anger start to swell up in Winston. When you are cheating, the guilt overtakes you to the point that you believe your mate or spouse is cheating as well, so you begin to act accordingly. Winston had guilt all over him, so he assumed I was doing it too, and he was right that time.

Kurt had no idea of my extracurricular activities such as getting high. But as we were on the phone, Winston was growing furious. His antics or his huffing and puffing did not intimidate me, so I continued our conversation. Kurt and I went from talking about the weather to talking about taking a cruise. Boy, did Winston get angry knowing another man was showing interest in me. I believe Kurt was just trying to butter me up so I wouldn't tell his girlfriend. He really didn't have to worry, but it was fun for me, stirring up Winston a bit. Finally, Winston couldn't take it anymore, and in one forceful slap across my face, he knocked the phone out of my hand and pulled the plug out of the wall. After a few more slaps from him, I ran out of the house to the next-door neighbor. I told her to call the police, and she did.

I peeked back in my screen door and saw Winston standing there. He had his back facing the door, so I tiptoed in and drew my arm way back, balled my fist, and thought of all the times he had beaten me.

In anger and with all my might, I punched him in his face. I knew he couldn't believe it because I never did anything like that before, but enough was enough. He had the nerve to have one of his friends down from New York with him, so I said, "You want to give your friend a show, let's make it a good one." After my punch had connected, he dropped his face into his hand and yelled out a cuss word and at that second I took off through the front door like lightning from the sky, because I knew what was coming next. He was about to wear my behind out, and I wasn't going to be stupid enough to stand there and take it, so I ran out and went back to the neighbor's house and waited for the police to come. I must have hurt him because he tried to have me arrested. The only reason they didn't take me was because he hit me first and admitted it, we both would have been arrested. I felt like I had won that one because after the police left, he didn't beat me again for a good while. I guess it dawned on him that I was tired and not going to take it anymore. When he got angry enough to want to beat me, I know he thought twice about it. I was not playing anymore. Yes, I was sick and drug addicted and desperate and naïve, but I was not going to allow him to beat me anymore. I was done.

He left that night and went back to New York, and I went back to using. The moment I knew he was gone; I made a phone call and was back to the same old same old—up all night using. I know God was with me because I was still alive. Winston had a reputation of being a bad boy people didn't play with him. He carried a gun, and when tempted he gave people the impression that he would use it.

Times weren't always so bad. A few weeks later my sister Liana tried to deter me from such activities. She called a talk show called The Jane Whitman Show and told them we were triplets and what our life was like growing up. We waited a couple days, and they called back and requested us to be guests on the show: my sister Liana, and our brother Levance, and me. At that particular time, our brother couldn't go, so Liana and I went. The show sent a black stretch limousine to my house to pick us up. That was our first time going to New York, and I knew that was something Liana really wanted to do, so I cleaned up and got ready for the trip to New York. When we got there, they took us straight to the green room. They had a lot for us to eat. It was an awesome experience. It took me away from the drugs for a little bit. It was truly out of sight, out of mind, and by the time we were finished eating, they were coming to take us to do our makeup and clothes. We wore the clothes they wanted us to wear, but when we were finished we had to return them to wardrobe, which we did. That was no problem because they said when we were finished they were paying us immediately. As soon as I heard money, I felt like I had to use the bathroom and vomit. I knew money meant drugs, drugs and more drugs.

We did the show and talked about what it was like being a triplet and how we loved each other and how awesome our mother was to have twins and triplets back to back only one year apart. But as we were doing the show, I remember feeling sick because my mind was back home on the drugs. I was so tired of feeling the anxiety and the fear from the paranoia, and there were many days when I lost all sense of reality because all I lived for was the drugs, and there was nothing anyone could do to change it. In my mind I was in a prison, and I had a life sentence. I was truly bound with no chance of parole. My life was drugs. I was a full-blown crack addict. People are under the impression that heroin takes a toll on the body, which is true, but the crack took a toll on my mind, which in fact then took a toll on my body. I couldn't stop. I tried, but all I lived for was the drugs.

As the show came to a close, I began to get excited because I had money—cold, hard cash to smoke without having to scheme, manipulate, or trick for it. We changed, they paid us, and then transported us all the way back to our houses. As soon as they dropped me off and then transported my sister to our mom's house. I was barely in the door, and I was calling Rob to come over. I wanted him to see how pretty I looked all made up. I left the makeup on from the show. I did feel pretty, and he came rather quickly. I was sure to tell him I had the cash and to just come. He gave me what I asked for and then left. I began to do what was the norm for me, and that was to sniff. Most of the time when I got the drugs from Rob, I sniffed and then at other times when it was already cooked up, I smoked it. And when I couldn't get either of the two, I smoked weed. I just always had to be under the influence. Perhaps I was trying to mask all the pain I felt from my past, present, and even my not-so-bright future. It was like I was in my own little world, all by myself with no one but my kids, and they were too young to understand. I thought I was getting away with something, but I wasn't. I was killing myself, slowly killing who I was, and killing my mind, killing my spirit, killing my self-esteem, killing every bit of who I really was.

After calling Rob over a couple of times, my money ran out, and I resorted to my usual behavior. I was driven by the addiction. I didn't see anything but drugs, but with no money I had no more drugs. Then my neighbor Thomas and his brother Luis started coming by late at night to see me. Luis owned a barbershop, so he had cash flow coming in and he liked me, so I quickly did the math. I hooked up with him. It helped that his pastimes were playing the lottery and sniffing cocaine and tricking, and for me two out of the three were fine. There were times when I would go to the bar and see him sitting there. He would buy me drinks and then propose that we go back to his barbershop for some after-hours pleasure. Though he was older, he was active. He was a business owner, and he was always well groomed. He was tall with a cute face and was mixed black and Puerto Rican. I was so sick I couldn't see straight or think straight, so if someone had money and was willing to spend it on me, I found something that was cute about him and held on to that so I wouldn't become disgusted and realize that what I was doing was wrong.

Addiction is no joke. People can get addicted to anything, and I mean that literally. Whether its illegal or prescription drugs, alcohol, cigarettes, sex, food, shopping, manipulation, control, money, power, beauty, other people, or love, there are many things that can become addictions. If you have an addictive personality or spirit, anything you touch has the potential to become an addiction. That was my issue. I used to blame it on the fact that I was an extremist, when in fact I simply had an addictive personality, or should I say it had me.

CHAPTER 9

Always Looking For Love

Wolves mated for life. Where was he? Where was the echo to her howl, her mate? Was there no other lone wolf, searching the hills for her? - Andrea Hurst

My drug use was far from over. With Winston in and out of my life, drugs became my lover. I began sleeping with men and doing other disgraceful things for money and drugs. I lived in a constant state of detachment. I had no feelings for these men, I never allowed myself to feel anything. I stayed focused on my goal. I didn't see myself as a prostitute or a whore, and I didn't feel sorry for myself either. I was just numb. There was something missing in my life, and I was looking for it. I was just a little girl who grew up too fast, and made some really bad choices, but I'm sure others who knew about my lifestyle had their own thoughts. I was so far gone; I didn't care what they thought. As long as my family and the people I loved didn't know about my lifestyle, I was fine. I did everything I could to keep them from knowing the truth. Although I'm sure they had an idea or heard rumors. Especially after my mom tried to help me.

One night Thomas said that his brother was over at his house, and he wanted to talk to me. I told him to send Luis over, so he went back and sent him over to me. That was just perfect. I didn't have any money or cocaine, so I was happy that he was coming over and I cleaned up a bit, not that it mattered. I had already found something to hold on to that I was attracted to. For some strange reason, I liked his nose and his lips, and I expressed that to him. I needed to find something attractive about him to make it all right. Then he would be more like a boyfriend than a trick. I asked if he had some cocaine, and he said yes. We went to the bottom room where I brought people to hang out. The kids were in their beds, and it was rather late. We sniffed until he had to leave. He offered me money to do things with him—sexual things—and I did that night. I was so high that it didn't matter what we did, because being high allowed me to disconnect myself from what was going on. When he was leaving he gave me about $300.

I just knew I had hit the jackpot. He left me with all that money and cocaine, and I began thinking I could really do it. I believed that was the life, all that money and drugs, just for a few minutes of sex. I didn't have to struggle to get it; it was basically at my fingertips. After that, I would just wait for him to go to his brother's from time to time, because that was the only safe way for him to see if Winston had come back in town or not. There was one time he came directly to my house without checking, and sure enough, Winston was there. He left after I let him know he couldn't come in. He was, in fact, my trick, but I liked him and was really beginning to feel something for him and his money and drugs. The lines between lover and trick began to get fuzzy and I wasn't sure what he was or what I wanted most. I didn't even know if he wanted me, or what his true feelings were.

Time passed, and that was life for me for a while. Then, I ran into a girl I met while attending a summer school class from back in the day, we hit it off great. Her name was Wanda White. She was taller than I and big, as I had been once upon a time before I lost some weight due to all the drug use. Eventually, I allowed her to move in with me. She was selling drugs, and I thought it was only a matter of time before she was going to get messed up too. The same way I started getting high and got addicted was the very direction she was headed in. But that wasn't something I could tell her. She would have thought I was jealous or crazy, so I kept it to myself, though occasionally I said something in the hope of deterring her from ending up like me.

Wanda would come and go with her boyfriend, a tall Jamaican man. At that time, I was trying to be normal, so I tried to date and began seeing a guy who went by the name of Locks. He was a friend of a friend, and he was really cute, an athletic build, dreadlocks, and very handsome. I couldn't figure out why he wanted me because I was messed up on drugs. I guess maybe it was something for him to do, so from time to time he and the others would come hang out with me, and we would smoke weed. I felt like that was much better and safer than smoking crack. On one particular night Locks took me upstairs, literally guiding me with his body. That was the first time a guy had ever done that. I loved the attention and affection; I craved it, because I had been missing it for a while. I wanted someone to want me with no strings attached. As he was guiding me with his body, he turned me around upstairs. We were in the hallway area of my house, and we began to kiss passionately. I was thinking how I could get used to that type of affection and passionate romance. It was amazing. He laid me down and slid on a condom, and we began to make love. I hadn't known him very long, but I could never recall being made to feel like such a lady as I did that night. He was a thug, but he treated me like I was his. Afterwards, we lay in each other's arms. It was the best feeling in the world, and not once did the desire for crack creep back on me. I just wanted that moment to last forever. Unfortunately, it didn't.

Locks had to leave a few hours later, and the next day I found out he had a girlfriend who was pregnant. I thought, "Are you kidding me?" I really liked him and thought he really liked me, but I was wrong. I found out about him when his girlfriend called my house and asked if I had something to do with him. I told her yes and explained everything from start to finish with no breaks or gaps. I was completely truthful and honest, but at the same time I was torn up inside, thinking, "What's wrong with me? Why can't someone love me just for me?" I felt stupid and worthless. I didn't know that they could sense my desperation and abused my vulnerability. After I told her, Locks went crazy. I guess she got on him, threw him out, and broke up with him. He got so irate he threatened me and called me all sorts of degrading names. There I was, thinking I had found somebody who wanted me for me and accepted me and liked me only for me, only to find out that I was just a pastime. He became so enraged that he said he was going to come at me. I didn't know what to think. I didn't try to break up his happy home intentionally. I thought he was single, so my finding out about his pregnant girlfriend was news to me. I was surprised by the whole thing, but at the same time I was torn on the inside and hurt. I felt deceived and used, and I hurt so badly. Nowadays this younger generation glorifies the "side chick" and they are fooled into being the other woman so that men can have their cake and eat it too. In the end you always end up feeling used, worthless, and unloved. Really only someone who is broken would agree to such a setup. The relationship just brings those feelings that are already there, to the surface, like a magnifying glass.

My next thought was cocaine. I went and got some from across the street and got high. Then who came knocking at the door? Locks!

He had a rather calm demeanor about him, almost too calm. I became very afraid. I cracked open the door to see what he wanted. I am telling you, it was my angel who was there with me holding that door, because when I saw his hands come up he had on hospital surgical gloves and was trying to barge his way through the door. Thank God I sobered up because instantly it dawned on me that he came to kill me and didn't want to leave prints anywhere. As he was trying to push the door in, it was unusual strength that rose up in me, and I pushed the door shut so he didn't get in. It was just my sons and I there, and all I could think about was protecting my children. Thank God I was still sober, and thank God he didn't get in. He truly came to kill me because of what I had told his girlfriend, which was the truth. He began to throw rocks at the house and yell names. I would yell back, "Yeah, you can call me what you want, but you still wanted me, and we still slept together!" Then he took a big rock and threw it through the living room window, just missing my baby son's head by inches. I immediately ran and picked my baby up off the couch and called the police. I had lost all sense of stability and structure as the mother I was supposed to be. I was still young and trying to a point to do what I thought was right, but mostly I was trying simply to live with no sense of direction. I had rejected my mother's help. I didn't even want to hear it because I thought I was grown up. I had my own place and paid my own bills to a certain point, so I felt my way was the right way. Of course, I was completely wrong. I know it was God's good grace that kept my children and me once again.

Obviously, that was the end of Locks and me. Though short-lived, he made me feel special, wanted and appreciated just for a moment. I told Wanda about it when she got in, and without hesitation she went crazy after seeing how scared we were and how dangerous it was for my kids. After the police took my statement and left, they pretty much took care of the rest. Locks was brought up on charges, but before that, my friend Wanda went down to his house, kicked the door in, and went crazy. She was big and not afraid, and she fought with him. But they didn't really want the trouble, so things calmed down after that, and that was the last of the whole issue with Locks.

I returned to the usual, very dysfunctional life I was living at the time. I was already feeling worthless, like I was never going to be wanted or appreciated for who I was before the addict, so things got worse. I would look forward to Luis coming. Yes, he was my trick, but when we were together he didn't make me feel worse than I already did, perhaps because we were both high and couldn't process things past the high. I just decided to settle for the hand that I felt was given me at the time. I thought I had no other choices. Of course, when I was under the influence, I lost all sense of morals and respect for myself, as well as good common sense. Luis started to come more often, and I really started to like him in some sick sort of way. When Winston, my kids' dad wasn't in town, Luis was my boyfriend. I began to have unprotected sex with him. As I said, I lost all good sense and morals. Here was this married man I am claiming to be my man, when he was really just a trick.

When I didn't have much money, not enough for cocaine or weed, I had to go out and seek my next victim—in a sense my next mark. I knew Luis liked to hang out at the bar, so I went there, hoping he would be there because if he was not, then I had to link up with a total stranger. That was dangerous because you just don't know people. Some are crazy, and some are straightforward. I hooked up with all kinds. When I saw Luis, I was relieved. I knew he wouldn't just leave me empty-handed. If he was there, he was drinking, and I knew what he wanted next, cocaine and sex. So he would buy me a drink, and we would talk a bit. Then he would gesture for me to meet him at his barbershop. I would leave before he did, and we would meet up outside the bar and go to his shop and sniff and then have sex. Afterwards I would go home after we had done all the cocaine he had, and that became my routine.

Often I would go out for some hours, and a lot of the time I left my kids alone. In some insane way, I was under the impression that they would be okay for a few hours. I can remember coming home and getting close to the house and just praying that they were okay. I didn't even realize what I was doing and subjecting them to, but when I got into the house and saw that they were fine, I would just hug them up so tight and thank God they were safe. The addiction truly had me. Once I was home with my children, I made sure they ate and took their baths. I hand washed their clothes in the tub and hung them outside to dry because our washer in the kitchen wasn't working. After I had done everything I could think of for them, I slept. I can't say how long, but I'm sure it was more than eight hours, and I would have my kids right with me sleeping or just sitting by me so I didn't have to worry about them. All the while I thought that was acceptable behavior. To be honest, I don't even know how things became so out of control. It was like my parenting skills and good judgment came and went. I certainly know God was looking out for us the whole time from the start to finish. I had exposed my children to a lot of harm and danger. At the time I couldn't see it, though. It was like I was blind. The drug use had blinded my judgment, my parenting skills, and my sense of righteousness.

One day I got all my rest, and the kids were content, as far as my mind would allow me to see. The kids were good, but I was not. I had no money, and it is unsettling to not be content under your own roof. So my mind began to race as it often did, and from out of nowhere the thought came to me to go see Luis unannounced. Things seemed strange because the lights to his shop were on but Luis wasn't coming to answer the door. I became angry and wanted to know what was going on, so I knocked harder. No matter what, I was not leaving. If he was in there getting high, he wasn't going to enjoy it because I was not leaving. He finally came and opened the door. Already paranoid and suspicious, I went to look around, and sure enough he had been in the back with a white girl, tricking. I yelled, "So, you couldn't get in contact with me, so you took another woman." Now he was a married man, so I don't know how I could possibly think he was devoted to me alone. But after glancing over the room, I saw powder on the table, along with some money. I said, "Okay, Okay, I see you are busy." I had already come up with a scheme to take it, so I buttered him up. One thing I was not into was being with women; that was out. Even now when I think back, I did everything else under the sun you can think of, but I refused to sleep with another woman. I would steal first, and I did. As I was leaving, I said, "Okay, Luis, when you finish with her, come find me. I will be waiting." On my way out the door, I swiftly swiped the cocaine he had offered me from the beginning, trying to keep me from causing a scene. In doing so, I also took the money that was meant for the girl in the back. And all I could think of was, him standing there with no pants on, and she was naked. He had the nerve to open the door, and that made me feel justified to steal.

The next day came. I knew he would be at the bar. I saw him, and I was a bit reluctant to go to him, but he was my source for drugs and money, which meant that I had to get over the fear and try my luck. When I approached him, he said in a calm voice, "You know you were wrong."

I replied, "Well, you shouldn't have had her there in the first place, so I took what really belonged to me." To my shock and amazement, he began to laugh and said to me,

"She was mad because of what you did." I dared him to say another word about that chick. I said that was just her bad luck and bad time. Then I began to laugh as hysterically as he was. After that, we never talked about it again. We went back to the shop and got high until we were finished. I then went home, and that was that.

Most of the time I had Luis's brother Thomas babysitting, and when I couldn't get a sitter, I left my children alone. But having Wanda there was good too. She was my sitter as well when she didn't have something to do. She often hung out at the bar across the street too. She liked a guy. I didn't know for sure if they were messing around with each other, but he was attractive, and he played with a band there. One day Wanda came to me and said she was not feeling well. I asked what was wrong, and she said the guy was dead. When I asked how, she said AIDS. My next thought was whether or not she had unprotected sex with him. But it was just that: a thought. I didn't want her to think I was getting in her business, so I let it go. As time went on, she began to come in all hours of the night. I hadn't seen Luis in some time, and when I had no access to the drug, I became irate, angry, frustrated, and irritable. So I told her she had to leave because my kids' father didn't want me having all sorts of people there. I knew what he really meant, but I used it to my advantage. I just didn't want to be around anybody but my kids. I was messed up mentally and emotionally.

A few days passed, and there I went again. I got much needed rest and ate a bit. I took care of my kids; I fed them, bathed them, and watched a movie with them. Then I was off again. As I was walking toward the barbershop, I came up with a plan to get money from him. I told Luis I was pregnant and he had to give me money for an abortion, as if I would ever do something like that. He panicked a bit because he was a married man. My plan worked brilliantly. I convinced him to give me money. It was half the money I asked for, but it was some money. After he gave me the money, we were together for a while using. I then left and went straight back to Carlito's Bar and bought some more cocaine. I didn't even want to wait for Rob to come, so I got the drugs and went home and used every bit of them.

When I was using, I felt like I was never getting enough, so I would sniff more, one hit after the next, until my chest felt like it was going to burst. I was so paranoid I would sit in the dark, scared to move, frozen with fear. My mind told me someone was coming after me, and you couldn't get me to think otherwise. As soon as that high would start to come down, my mind went from someone hurting me to a need to have more, and that was the cycle until it was all gone. It's tiring just thinking about it, but that was my life. After I used everything, then I would smoke the weed to deter me from thinking about the fact that I didn't have any more cocaine.

I started feeling really tired and didn't think about it much at first, but my period stopped coming. I knew I was pregnant again, so I went to Luis and told him. He swore up and down I was lying, but that time I wasn't. I took a pregnancy test, and, sure enough, I really was pregnant. But because I had faked a pregnancy before to get money, he thought I was lying and refused to give me any money. I thought, "Oh no. Now I'm really stuck."

It had been a long while, but Winston came back. Now he found things missing from the house because when I didn't have any money left and couldn't get the drugs, I began to sell things from the house. I know he was hurt, but that was the life of an active addict. It was not pretty. Addiction never is. By any means possible, I had to get the drugs. All I lived for was the drugs. It was insanity. I can't tell you I saw it coming, because I didn't. Things just spiraled and got worse for me. I had to go to food pantries for food because I was selling the food stamps. I set aside the bill money that I got from welfare, but after my spare money was gone, I went straight into the rent money and any other money I had left. It all went up my nose. Then I began to get nosebleeds and knew I couldn't keep doing it that way because I was burning the inside of my nose. I was afraid of creating a hole in my nose, so I began to smoke when I could.

After Luis denied me the money, he stopped messing with me. At the time I didn't care. I just went to the next means of getting drugs, so I began to hang over at the bar a lot and met a Dominican guy. He was tall, and he sold cocaine. I was pregnant, but these were the early stages of pregnancy, so nobody knew. He treated me well. He was cute and tall, and his place of business was the bar. That was good because it was right across the street from my house and I didn't have to stay away from home as much. After hanging out in the bar, he would come over and give me some blow, and we would have sex—with protection of course. Afterward, he would give me one or two bags, or if he had extra at the end of the night, what he had left was mine. I actually liked him, but again I was kidding myself to think he really liked me for me. The sex I gave him was good to him not to me as a person. I gave a little and got a little—even trade, or so I thought.

One night I had left the kids in the house by themselves, and of all nights Winston decided to show up. I was not there, but he knew where to find me. He sent his friend he came down with to the bar to call me. He was already in the house. He got in through the broken window that was still there from when Locks broke it. When I got to the door, I was sure we were about to fight. But instead of a fight, it was more of a lecture. I knew Winston was tired and just didn't know what to do. He was right. I was wrong to leave the kids, but I was so out of control I mixed up reality with some other kind of world. He had some beer. He drank Budweiser by the case and that was his favorite pastime. I stayed and drank with him and came down from the speed I had gotten up to. When I was on cocaine, I was going a hundred miles per hour. My thoughts were constantly racing. I was paranoid; anxiety took total control over my mind. I was messed up.

Some hours went by, and he and I talked. I explained that it was not intentional, that he was never there and as soon as he left things got crazy again each and every time. He didn't understand, I could tell. I also told him it was so hard to stop, but I would try. In fact, I did try, but the desire for the drug was stronger than any other feeling I have ever experienced in my life. I could not stop. I was bound. That drug had me.

Since things were calm, I saw it as the perfect opportunity to tell him about the pregnancy and to be honest. When I told him, he said if we were going to stay together, I had to get an abortion. He was serious. That went against everything I believed. Even in the state I was in, I was against it, but he persuaded me and led me to believe there was no other way. I had to abort my baby, so I went along with his idea. The next day we made an appointment. He gave me the $100 consultation fee for the abortion and went with me. They explained everything to me, but that was not well with me. I was thinking that no matter what, I could not kill my baby. I didn't have my right mind, but I knew I didn't want to kill my baby.

After the appointment, Winston had to go somewhere for a couple days. I was supposed to go back to the Women's Center for the abortion, and the initial $100 would be applied to the total cost. I purposely missed that appointment. I didn't care if Winston was going to lose that $100 or not. I just could not do it, and, thank God, I didn't. I was messed up, but I just couldn't do it. Winston became upset when I told him, and we became more distant than ever before. He didn't want to give me another dime, so I ended up being evicted. I didn't have the money to pay and couldn't get it, so I had to leave. I know my neighbor or somebody was happy for that. I don't know who it was, but somebody had put some corn on my doorstep. I guess that was a form of voodoo to try to get me to leave. I was paranoid, so if that was voodoo, all they had to do was ask me, and I would have gone. I was not playing with voodoo or the people behind it. I was already messed up in the head. The final straw was when I saw a black snake crawling outside on my porch shortly after the corn appeared. I wanted to leave, I just didn't have the means or the common sense to go and look for another apartment before getting put out of that one. So I took what I could, along with my kids, and went back home to my mom's house. I had no other choice.

CHAPTER 10

Slippery Slope

Don't stay too long in the shame-filled grounds of relapse. Fertile soil awaits your return and your recovering. ~ Holli Kevinley

My mom had relocated to Allentown. She said she was tired of Bethlehem, and she was beginning to come out of her shell a bit. I believe my mom was afraid of change. We all know change is inevitable; it's going to happen with or without us. But change can sometimes be very uncomfortable if we are not prepared for it. Mom went to extremes when she got fed up with a situation. In other words, when her back was against the wall, my mom came out swinging. She challenged herself a lot of times without even knowing it. For example, she stepped out on faith and moved to Pennsylvania from Florida, she gave birth to us triplets after being diagnosed with cervical cancer, and when she had enough of the welfare system and the projects, we took what we could carry and walked away from the government assistance. She also chose to stay with my dad through all the years of his drug addiction and abuse, and then when she knew she had to leave, she left without knowing how it was going to turn out, and we followed. But she believed we were going to be just fine.

She got an apartment on Seventh Street, not the best part of town, but she did it on her own, and my sister Buffy was right there with her. My mother did a good job with us, and I know it baffled her how I could end up addicted to drugs after she gave us all the love a mother could possibly give her children. I believe my mom was numb to my behavior; she didn't know how she could help me. I didn't know how to go about telling her I needed her help. I was stuck, my mind was under arrest and I believed I had no way of getting free. I didn't really know who I could reach out to. I had hurt so many people by betraying their trust and because of all of my careless behavior I stayed in a constant state of confusion.

After going to stay with her, it soon became clear that things were still out of control. I hid it for a while, but then I started to stay out, and she became a regular babysitter. But that didn't last for long. Mom wasn't stupid, she knew what I was doing wasn't right, so she stopped babysitting. I couldn't take her rules, and I thought I was always right. I would soon have to admit that she was right. I gave birth to my fourth son and found out that my son had drugs in his system, which was a wake up call for me. They didn't take my baby but I had to clean up which I did for a while. That didn't last long because I was an addict and I wasn't ready to be clean. I hadn't made the decision, the decision was made for me, and I had to do things my way. I was not a fan of rules and boundaries, and I didn't think they applied to me or mattered, but my mother still insisted on telling me what to do. Even though it was for my best interest, I didn't want to hear it. I took my infant son and moved in with Liana. My mom still had my oldest son, while my other two sons were visiting their father, Winston. Their temporary visit turned into an extended stay because I was unable to take care of them in the state of mind that I was in.

I was back to feeding my addiction and soon I was leaving my one son that I did have left, with Liana because all I was focused on was the drugs. I had no mind for anything else. The drugs had a hold on me; I tried and tried hard to stop, but I didn't stop. In fact, things only got worse.

People around began to notice and tell me I had to do something, so I did. I got some information on a rehab, but I didn't know what I was going to do with my children. I knew I had to get clean, though. Winston came down after I expressed to him my need to clean myself up, and through a friend of a friend, we found placement for my children so I could complete the rehab. My youngest child at the time went to stay with Lilly. She was a woman that was known for helping young mothers with their children. I was introduced to her by one of Winston's friends. Laquan was still with my mom, Winston finally stepped up and we decided that it would be best for him to keep our two sons with him and his family in New York. Winston questioned the paternity of our second son, my third, until we eventually had a paternity test proving him to be his father. I did not have a choice if I wanted a chance. Either I would be placing them with people I knew and trusted, or children's services would place them in stranger's homes.

Being in rehab was like something I watched on television, I couldn't understand how I allowed things to get that bad. I learned that there were deep rooted issues within me that were never fixed and I used the drugs as medicine, but all they did was make me worse. That particular rehab experience was the beginning to a series of short lived institutional care. A few I left and a few I stayed but afterwards I went back to the same behaviors. While in rehab I told them what they wanted to hear and did all I could to avoid any delays on my home care. It wasn't until later that I found that in order to get and stay clean you had to want to; it was not something you could fake.

While in those facilities you have to meet at an appointed time in small groups, some of us women were on medication for mental health issues. I was diagnosed as being Bipolar and I did suffer from extreme mood swings and even on occasion anxiety attacks, but that was not as bad as symptoms of the addiction. When I was there I took the medication they prescribed and appeared to be getting myself together but as soon as left I was back at it again; everything I thought I learned was gone, but not forgotten. While going from rehab to rehab I was picking up seeds and tools to use for when I was ready to quit. Many times because of our limited understanding we may feel that we are being punished when in fact there are consequences to our actions. Until we are ready to change those actions, the cycle and consequences continue. I had to be so broken so desperate and so done that finally God could not only get my attention but keep my attention.

Addiction is like an old raggedy t-shirt that looked bad and smelled bad, but it was familiar and because it was familiar it was comfortable and because it was comfortable I kept going back to it because I thought in some ways it was all I had. It was my friend. It became my false sense of security that allowed me to be numb, feeling nothing when times got rough and life became tough. My addiction became more than a ragged t-shirt with holes to me; it became my comfort and my answer to having to deal with anything I encountered. I was indeed addicted to men, drugs, attention, sex, relationships, and later on material things, which then led to control.

I didn't have any kids with me after the rehab. I was supposed to go back and get them, but I came out of the rehab worse than when I went in. One thing I did come to realize is that "trying" to get clean was for my family, but actually "getting" clean was for me. My mom couldn't make me quit, my kids couldn't make me stop, Winston couldn't make me stop, and my sister Liana couldn't make me stop. Only I could make me stop, and I am telling you, I was not ready to stop. I knew my kids were safe and it hurt me to be out there like I was, but I could not stop. I wanted to do better. I wanted to be a good mom like my mom was to me, but I could not stop. There was nothing stopping me from becoming a full-fledged crack addict as soon as I got any money to purchase the drug. Things had spun way out of control. Each and every time I thought about the crack, I immediately had to go to the bathroom to have a bowel movement. The anxiety became so intense it was unbearable but never to the point that I would stop. I kept using and just chalked the bathroom experiences up as a symptom of drug addiction.

It was 1995, the worst year of my life. So many things went wrong. My kids were gone, my mom and family didn't know where I was. I didn't have a job and wasn't stable enough to get welfare. I had no means of income or a way of getting the drugs so I resorted back to the oldest profession in the book, which was prostituting. It was not something I planned and it really started with Rob and his brother. I was desperate for the drugs and didn't have another way. I would single out a guy at a stop light or at a store and ask for a ride. After I got in the car I would then feel him out a little bit to see if he was thinking what I was thinking. I was also afraid, because I heard the horror stories of women getting hurt and even killed. I ignored these thoughts and did it. I preferred the drug dealers at night because I knew some of them and it was always with protection. At night, when no one was around to see, was the perfect time to proposition a drug dealer they almost never said no. That was my hustle for a while.

It's hard to admit, but I was standing around waiting for tricks and random guys to come pick me up so I could get the money to get high. I had run out of options. I believed that it was all I had left, because I wasn't ready to stop using. I had already lost my self-respect, my dignity, my children, and my family. I hated when the sun would come up because then I would be exposed. Night was best for me because it hid my shame and covered up my guilt and allowed me to stay in that bondage. There is a Scripture in the Bible that speaks of this very thing. In The Bible, John Chapter 3 verse 20 says, "For everyone practicing evil hates the light and does not come into the light, lest his deeds should be exposed." That was my life. I was not only sick and in active addiction, I was in trouble and I knew how deep I was sinking. I thought the life I was living had no escape, so I just kept going with the flow. My mind was held captive by a false sense of control. I thought I was handling things, but I was wrong.

I had forgotten all morals and values. I had hit rock bottom, and it didn't matter to me how far gone I was. My everyday goal had become to seek out drug dealers and tricks to get more drugs. I was skinny and malnourished. I was often hungry, but my appetite for the drugs was more than for food. No matter how high I was getting or how fast I was smoking, I was never satisfied. I kept saying to myself "just one more," and that one more became a thousand more. I just couldn't get enough. My heart could literally beat in my chest like it was about to run out of there, and I would just smoke more, but even then God was keeping me because I should have been dead. I had many overdoses but never went to the hospital. When I took too much too fast, I would take the hit, and my mind would go blank, and all I could do was run hard and run fast, trying desperately to find my breath, but even it was far from me. I had accepted the idea of death, but I would never commit suicide. Just like abortion, it was against my beliefs and everyone has a line they just won't cross. That lifestyle was as close as I would get to suicide, but there were times when I thought that death had to be better than the life I was living.

One day I walked around for hours. Things were slow, and I had nothing to do but walk around. I came across a Hispanic man, and I initiated the conversation. I said, "Hi, how you doing?" We began to talk, and he invited me into his apartment. He was very nice, unusually nice, so I thought it was going to be easy money and afterwards I would go get some crack. He offered me some tea and something to eat. I guess he could see I was hungry, and I was. But every time I thought about the drugs, my appetite would leave, no matter how hungry I was. The drugs were my life. I refused the tea and food. I was ready to get on with it, so I could leave and find the drug dealer who would give me the good deal. So I sat down next to him and asked him what was up and what he wanted to do. He looked at me in my eyes. I was baffled, but I was determined to get that money. Then he said to me, "I can't sleep with you." I thought, Why not? I'm of age. But to my shock and amazement, he then said to me, "I can't sleep with you because I have AIDS." I sat there dumbfounded, but it didn't scare me for some reason. I didn't even leave immediately.

I then said, "Okay." I took his face, kissed him on the cheek and said to him, "I'm not afraid of you, but thank you." Suddenly, I got my appetite back, and I just wanted to eat and gather my thoughts. After eating and talking to him for a while, I left. Every now and again after that day, I would see him, almost like he was watching me, but I wasn't afraid. I would wave and keep moving. That was my last encounter with him. I was still out there with no sense of direction and no other thoughts. The crack was my life.

I was a bit tired, and I was reaching out for help. Not knowing what else to do, I called Winston. Winston seemed to want to be there, because despite the condition or state of mind I was in, I was still the mother of his children. So I called him. He seemed like the only one I really had. I didn't consider anyone else. My mom was there, but she didn't know how to help me because I was too far-gone. Most of the time I stayed away from my sisters because I didn't want them to see me that way. With all of the shame, the lack of respect for myself, and the low self-esteem the drugs only made everything worse. When I hurt, I wanted drugs. When I was confused, I wanted drugs. When I felt alone, I wanted drugs. When I was tired, I wanted drugs. I wanted drugs all the time to mask different feelings I just didn't want to feel. My escape was drugs. Praise God that's all it was because it could have been worse—something I couldn't come back from. But back then I was lost and didn't know I could be found

So I called Winston, and we talked for a few minutes. We thought it would be best if he took me away from Allentown. We thought that if I moved away from the drugs, I would get clean and change my life. That was the plan, the solution. It had to work because I knew the places to go to get the drugs. I knew the people to get them from. We thought moving to a different place had to be the answer. Winston came down from New York, and I packed my things and told everyone I was leaving. But in the meantime, I had gone out on a binge. All I kept thinking about was the fact that I was getting ready to leave and I was going to get high until then. I didn't care about anyone or anything. The more I was out there, the worse I got. I was losing myself more and more each day. I was falling and couldn't get back up.

I didn't have to think about my children because they were already in safe places. I didn't realize how my children saved my life all those years before. I believe that is why Winston never took the boys from me. I was out there, but I wouldn't go to far, because I knew they needed me, and depended on me, because I was all they had. With them being gone, all I could think about was getting high. When I woke up each day, my first thought was smoking, and before I went to sleep, if I happened to sleep, my last thought was getting drugs. It was truly as if every bit of values and morals and self-respect had been ripped from my mind totally. It was like I never had any good sense, when in reality the drugs, the addiction, stole all of that from me. Every bit of the woman, daughter, mother, and sister that I was I exchanged for a numbing feeling that didn't last; to keep it going I had to keep chasing it.

I was too out of control to stay with Liana. I was so embarrassed and ashamed I couldn't let Liana see how bad I was getting. I left even though she never judged me or cast me out. In fact, she protected me and fed me when she could. I never really stayed in one place for very long; only a couple of nights at a time and if I stayed in one place for more than a week it's because I had no choice. When I would retreat back to her house it was for refuge and rest. I knew I would be safe, but the Ivana she grew up with and the person I was turning into were two different people. I grew very tired and I went to stay with my mom on South Seventh Street in Allentown.

* * * * * * *

After I was well-rested and got my second wind, I was ready again. No matter how my mother tried to help me, all I could think about was the drugs. My mind was always racing with only one focus, drugs. A friend of my sister and I had moved across the street from my mom. She was young, and she had a lot of people in and out, a lot of drug dealers. I wanted to hang out too. I was on drugs, but I cleaned up to make myself look like I fit in. I was hanging across the way from my mom's apartment, and my friend Rachael allowed me to smoke in her house. I don't know why but she did. I had run out of drugs, but a male friend of hers also used to hang there. His name was Blakks. As an addict you act quickly without thinking about the consequences. You get to the point to where you constantly engage in mind games. I played on people and learned how to take from them without violence or hassle. My line was, "I will sell for you and get the money back to you when I finish." It seemed to work often. Blakks fell for it.

My intentions really were to sell the drugs and smoke only my cut. But when I got started, I couldn't stop. I stayed there in that room and smoked until the entire pack was gone, maybe about $40 worth of crack cocaine. I owed him $40 and as I was sitting there toward the end, in my mind saying, "Just one more hit. I will break the bags down smaller and get his money." The bag got smaller and smaller down to the last hit. Then I started to almost panic, so I took the last hit so I wouldn't be afraid anymore. However, as soon as the feeling wore off, the panic returned because I didn't have $1, nor did I have any means of getting him his money. All I could do was sit there in that room, try-ing to figure out what I was going to do. Then I heard a knock on the door. I had the door locked, and my mom lived just across the street. All kinds of things were running through my mind, but I was sitting there so frozen with fear, there was nothing I could do. So I open the door and suddenly, out of nowhere he punched me in the face and be-gan to beat me and kick me. I know everyone in the house heard what was going on, but no one would help. I was being beaten for smoking up this man's drugs. But it seemed as if I were numb or something, because I felt shame more than pain. I was being beaten for the crack I had smoked up, when once upon a time I was selling it and watching stuff like that happen to other people. I was once beating someone who did the same thing to me with Winston's drugs. The tables certainly had turned. In fact, I could remember when I was selling; I looked at buyers and wondered why they were using this. I looked at them, almost mocking them in a sense. I went from laughing at them to being laughed at myself.

The whole time I was learning humility—the hard way. I couldn't believe what I had allowed myself to go through or get involved in, but the drugs had me. I will say, though, if it wasn't for God that man would have killed me regardless of the amount, it was the principle of the matter. The bottom line was that I stole from him and now I had to pay for it. After the beating, I took time coming out of the room. I wanted to make sure the coast was clear. I didn't want to get another beating, so I ran across the street to my mom's house. By that time the high was completely down, and I was sober and just wanted to be safe and with my mom. I felt safe in my mom's unconditional love. I know if she could have, she would have made that whole thing stop, but it was a process I had to endure. I had to go through it and overcome it because there was a lesson I had to learn as a result of that way of life. I did learn it, but it took a long time to do so.

I got some rest, and then I called Winston. I had become bold and overcome with anger. I told Winston that he had put his hands on me; he became angry and wanted to come that night. He said we were going to the reggae club, and if we saw him there, we were going to handle it. Later that night, we were at the club. When I clean up, I clean up well. I can hide things well, so I was presentable enough to be there, and Winston wasn't having it any other way.

Then I saw Blakks, the guy who beat me up. Now when I told Winston the story, I might have left out a few minor details, like why Blakks hit me, simply because of the shame and embarrassment of having smoked up the boy's drugs. Winston asked me if that was him, and I said yes. He then instructed me to punch him in the face and then Winston would do the rest. Like an idiot, I did it, and it was the dumbest thing I could have done. My mind-set wasn't right, so as in so many other things and issues in my life at the time, I didn't think about any consequences.

I approached him as he was leaning on a car. I remember turning the ring on my finger around. I said to him, "Remember when you hit me and beat me?" I was building up the nerve to do it, trying to fight through the fear and look big and bad. I said, "Oh, so you want to fight. I bet you won't hit me again." He said some words. I balled up my right hand into a fist and pulled it way back and drew it up to his face with a force that came from some unknown place in me. As my punch connected with his face, things sped up, and everything happened quickly. He hit the ground but came back up with a straight razor and sliced me in my face. My two sisters were there, Buffy and Liana. I didn't know where Winston went, but I held my face in disbelief. I didn't expect that and I didn't see it coming. Before I knew it, he came back around the back of me, trying to slice my neck from behind. Liana broke a bottle, ready to attack the next person who was trying to jump in, because he had two of his friends with him. Winston ran Blakks down, but I don't know what happened. The ambulance was called, and they took me to the hospital. That is how I know God is good and shielded me even then. When I got to the hospital, they stitched my face with thirty stitches and my left ear lobe with a few more. After examining my cuts, they discovered that what looked like a cut on my neck was just a scratch; the blade didn't go through it. My face and my ear were cut wide open, but my neck where my jugular vein is located had only a scratch. Praise God! I thank Him because I am alive when I should have been dead. God kept me.

After that, we decided that now would be the best time for me to leave the area, no more delays. Winston came and he finished packing all my things, and took me to a halfway house in New York. His brother was a minister, and he worked and lived there. He ran the center and had an apartment on the ground floor. His name was Dean.

Everyone thought that was going to be the best thing for me. Change is good but only when you are ready for it. If you are not ready for change, things will remain the same or just get worse. At least that was my experience thus far. After a while, things got worse for me.

I distinctly remember an encounter I had before I moved to New York. When I knew I was going, I broadcast it. I was so happy I was going to get better. Things were perfect, I told a guy I was buying drugs from that I was going to New York and it was going to be better there. He got a look in his eyes like worry. I didn't read too much into it, but then he looked directly into my eyes and said to me, "If you go to New York, you are going to become a bigger crack-head." I looked at him and told him, first of all, I was not a crack-head and, second, things were going to be better because I was getting away from these streets and the drugs. Little did I know drugs were everywhere. In fact, exactly what that guy said would happen actually did, (he planted a negative seed and I received it clearly). Those words haunted me for as long as I could remember regardless of the amount of denial I was truly in. It all comes down to one thing, you can take an addict out of a drug area but unless the mindset is renewed or the problem addressed you only end up taking the addict as well as the problem with you, the person is still addicted. It didn't matter where I went, I would find the drugs by any means necessary. And when I found them in New York, they were far cheaper. I could actually buy a hit for $2. I went up there with the intention to do better but had not yet learned the tools needed to change the mindset that kept me wanting the drugs and that lifestyle.

The plan was for me to stay in the halfway house just a short time. I was supposed to be going to rehab in a couple of weeks in upstate New York. We thought all was going to be okay. Winston loaded me up with everything he thought I was going to need. He just knew that would be the solution, and so did I, but we were wrong. When we got to New York, he dropped me off at the place where his brother worked. The halfway house/shelter was for young kids who needed help. Some were homeless, some were homosexuals who were rejected by their families, and some, like me, just needed help. No one knew why I was there except for Winston and his brother Dean. I got situated and settled in, and things were going well. I was not using, and I didn't know anyone. It was supposed to be a new beginning, a fresh start in life. I had everything I needed. My kids were safe, and I was stable, or so I thought. Things seemed great. However, after Winston dropped me off, he left again and went back to his other family. Now we both were there in New York, but it didn't matter much because I was a part-time lover. He was there with his other family way more, and really all I wanted was a good life. The drugs had me bound me, and I didn't know how to make this new life happen. I was still young, and I was so confused.

Being confused wasn't a good thing for me because soon after the confusion came the racing thoughts. I began to take walks and look around the place and meet people. The addiction had started to take over and control my mind. I began to think fast. I had a couple bucks on me. I had not been using, so everyone thought it was safe for me to have money. Deep down I knew it was dangerous. I started asking questions, and soon I found the drugs. They were much cheaper, so I would just buy a couple because I didn't want anyone to know I was using. I would go into the bathroom at the center and use them, which we often referred to the halfway house as a shelter as well as a center.

After a while my roommate at the shelter moved out of the room that I was in and moved in with her girlfriend in the shelter. So I ended up having my own room. I then began smoking in my room and stopped caring as much. Shockingly, I didn't get caught. However, one day I started arguing with the girl who had moved out of the room I was in. I said some hurtful things, and so did she. She then called me a crack-head. I yelled back, "I don't use crack anymore!" I immediately went into defense mode. But it was just out of coincidence that she called me a crack-head, because she didn't even know I was using crack or that I had a crack addiction. The director, in fact, told me she was only saying things to hurt me. I began to cry and knew I couldn't stay there. Winston heard about everything, and his brother did too. Dean said if my urine was dirty I had to leave the center/shelter, and sure enough it was dirty, so I had to leave.

Winston was furious, but I was now his responsibility. He couldn't take me back to Allentown, so he started the process of making the necessary arrangements for me to go to rehab in upstate New York, once again thinking the farther away from drugs I was, the better things would be for me. In the meantime, he took me to a friend's house in the Bronx. Their way of living was a bit different from how I was raised. There were many rules. I had to get up early every morning, I couldn't sleep in at all, and I couldn't stay out late which was a familiar rule, one my own mom enforced. I was trying to fit in. I knew they didn't really like me. In fact, I didn't even like me. I just didn't know what to do, so I was just going with the flow.

One day Winston decided to take me back over by the center. We weren't supposed to stay. He was just visiting his brother, so things were cool. I hadn't been using, and I looked good and felt good. After being there a while, Winston left me. I was bored and had nothing to do, so my mind started to race once again. I left and found some drugs, but I didn't have anywhere to use them. So I found different people who used and before I knew it hours had passed. I was across town, far from where I started out. I ran into a guy who was a drug dealer. He was fine, and I looked good too. I was cleaned up and fresh. I went back to this guy's house with him, and he propositioned me. He said if we had sex, he would give me crack. He was cute and in my sick mind I was thinking, you don't even need to pay me, you look so good. Then he said to me, "If I show you something, are you going to get scared." When I said I wouldn't, he came back in with a boiling pot full of crack cocaine. I thought, "Oh no. This is it. I've hooked up with this kingpin. Any minute somebody is going to kick his door in trying to rob him, and that is going to be it for me." The amount of crack he showed me caused me to panic, but my desire for the drugs outweighed the paranoia, at least for a while.

When we got intimate, he gave me a bag and then another. He was giving me from the stash he had already made up. He was practically feeding me the drugs the whole night. We were intimate three or four times, but he kept giving me the drugs. Each time I took a hit I became more paranoid. Finally, I went and hid in his twelve year old daughter's room, where she was asleep. I knelt in her room until the high went away and I felt safe again.

When the sun began to rise, he told me I had to leave because his daughter had to go to school soon. I asked if I could take a bath first, and he said yes. I didn't have any fresh clothes to wear, so I took off the brand-new clothes Winston had given me, and the man gave me some raggedy clothes to put on. The shirt had a hole in the belly. I didn't know how bad I looked nor could I even process it. I had been up all night high and had no sense of how to handle that particular situation; sleep deprivation had begun to set in. My coordination was off. I was a mess and couldn't even see it. He gave me money for the subway I didn't even know where I was, so I got directions back to the Center and tried to follow them. My coordination was off so badly I was staggering, and because of that one of my shoes fell on the track as I was switching trains, and I just didn't have the energy or sense to get it, so I went the rest of the way barefoot. Finally, after what seemed like hours and hours, I got on familiar ground and got back to the Center.

Dean called Winston, and Winston came immediately. Without speaking to me, he began to beat me like I stole something. I tried to fight back, but he picked me up and took me back to the Bronx. Just as we were going over the Brooklyn Bridge, he punched me in the face without warning, and there was nothing I could even do about it. I didn't know what to do. I was sick in my mind I couldn't understand why I was doing what I was doing. I had lost my mind. I tried to be normal, but it didn't last because I was stricken with the disease of addiction. When he got me back to his friend's house, he tried to fight me some more. By then, I had had enough. Yes, I messed up, but I wasn't going to allow him to continue to beat on me. So I got right back in his face and said, "Try me!" I even pulled a knife. I was bleeding from my nose and mouth, and I was tired. I just could not take anymore. Finally, after everything was all settled, the lady of the house said I had to leave. She didn't want me there, and I couldn't blame her for that. The life I was living was unacceptable. I was the only one who didn't know it.

Winston got me a room in a rooming house across the way. I was tired and hurt and beat down physically, mentally, and emotionally, when I would lie down, I slept for days. All I know is Winston said he would be back. He brought me food and came when he wanted sex, but pretty much I couldn't leave. It was like prison. He even went so far as to take my clothes and my shoes to try to stop me from leaving. It worked for a little while, but I managed to befriend the owner of the house. She gave me some clothes and some shoes, and I was off again.

I walked until I found the young dealers. They were cute too, which made it easier for me to get into my manipulation mode, and I ended up charming them for the drugs. I didn't have much money, we worked out other deals, and sure enough the guys began to come looking for me. Surprisingly, they never came when Winston was there.

CHAPTER 11

Big City Streets

The world is a dangerous place to live; not because of the people who are evil, but because of the people who don't do anything about it. - Albert Einstein

When it came time for me to go to rehab, Winston drove me. I knew he was happy to get me off his hands for a while. I was happy too, and I was tired. We drove six hours to upstate New York to a rehab place for girls. After about the third day there, I wanted to leave. Another girl who came in wanted to leave too, and a few other girls as well, but only the two of us actually ended up leaving. We had no money and had to leave all our possessions behind because we couldn't manage them. The girl, named China, and I hitch-hiked all the way back to the Bronx. She said I would have a place to stay and she wouldn't leave me and we would be fine. A group of white guys who were drinking picked us up and took us back to the Bronx to her family's place. But as soon as we got to a place she knew, she took me in one house and left me there and never came back for me. I was the silly one, taking the word of an addict. How many times had I done the same thing? Tell people what they want to hear with no intention of following through.

I was on my own. I would have sold the jewelry I had on to try to continue the high, but there was none left. I didn't know anything about where I was, so I didn't even want to sell my body. I wanted to get back to familiar ground, some place I knew, and that was Manhattan. The man at the house where China left me, helped me get to Manhattan, and from there I had no one. I was alone. I had only that monkey on my back that wouldn't let up. It wouldn't allow me any space. I knew that I needed time to think, time to heal, part of me wished I had stayed in rehab, but that disease had me bound. No matter how I tried to escape it, it was like trying to run from my shadow. The enemy had me in his grip and was looking to kill, steal, and destroy the person God called me to be. The enemy didn't want me free, and I wasn't sure I knew what freedom was anymore. My mind was a mess;

I was constantly in a state of confusion, fear, anxiety, depression, guilt, or regret. It seemed like the more I tried to do right, the more I ended up doing wrong. I knew it was probably a bad idea to leave rehab with that girl; I allowed her to influence me, I didn't see at the time that she was just a distraction, and all she did was use me for company. But on that journey, which was one I chose, I could have ended up anywhere. I am just thankful I didn't end up dead. God kept me yet again.

I was finally on some familiar ground. I felt better when I arrived, but I'm not sure why because I still didn't have anyone. Winston didn't even know that I had left rehab, and I was afraid to tell him. I didn't want to get beat up, nor did I want to disappoint my family because I knew he would have phoned them after finding out. Therefore, I just stayed out there walking around, not really knowing what to do or where to go, just looking for an opportunity I guess. When a guy approached me, my mind started racing. I was just looking to do what came next. I didn't have any plans or money. A big black guy came up to me and asked me what was up, and I responded by saying nothing was up and that I was just chilling. I said I got locked out of my house and was just hanging out. I had to come up with a quick lie; it was the only thing I was good at. We kicked a few words back and forth, and he said he was just hanging out and didn't really have anything to do. He asked if I just wanted to hang out with him for a while, and we headed toward the house where he was staying. I began to feel very comfortable with him. I guess I was just looking for some safety. I knew what I was doing was dangerous, but the idea of potential drugs and the high took precedence over my own safety.

After a while I began to tell him what really happened. He offered to take me over to his place in the projects, so I went. He was a different kind of man. He was quiet. He seemed to be shy and timid. After talking for a while, I let him know I got high. It seemed like everyone back then was doing it, or maybe it was just who I was associating myself with just like what I saw as a child in the projects I grew up in. The drugs were the center of my world, so I clung to people who either sold them or used them. He bought me some drugs, and we were there hanging out, but as we talked, things seemed different. I noticed he was taking a liking to me and was acting as if he was really concerned about me. After getting high a few more hours that night and being so tired from the hitchhiking from upstate New York to the Bronx and from the Bronx to Manhattan and Harlem, he allowed me to stay with him. There was no sex that night, just sleep.

After I woke up, he took me to get something to eat. I was hungry, but in that type of lifestyle, I was no stranger to hunger. We ate and started walking around, talking. I did not really know my next move. I was just going with the flow. Wherever the drugs took me, I went. It got that bad, all because of some choices I made at a very young age. I can't help but think that if I had just listened to my mother and honored her like the Bible says, I wouldn't have been in the predicament that I allowed myself to be in. It would be all too easy to say the devil did it, but I made the choices and the decisions. Sure, I was tempted, but I knew right from wrong and because I didn't resist temptation, that is where I ended up, in the arms of a stranger so far away from home. I was in a mental, spiritual, and physical prison and I didn't know how to escape. I couldn't help but wonder how long that cycle would repeat itself?

We headed back to the projects, where he was staying with a lady named Cookie. She and I got along well. In fact, I usually got along pretty good with people, mostly because I was alone out there and I couldn't afford to get anyone upset with me. Perhaps that was where my need to please people was developed. I also had trust issues, so if I allowed people to feel comfortable around me they would let down their walls first, and I could determine if they were worthy of my trust.

I had eaten and was well rested, so the only other thing for me to do was what I was used to doing at the time, getting high. And, shockingly, he was fine with that. Indeed, if you show me your company and friends, I can tell you who you are. I put myself in that environment and had no way of escaping it. I was locked up in my mind, and the chains on my shackles stretched only as far as the next hit. He bought me more drugs, and that time I had to put up or get out, so I did what I had to do to stay and be safe while doing it. Then the money ran out. He didn't have any more drugs or money, so I left.

I started meeting other guys, mostly drug dealers. I walked aimlessly up and down Seventh Avenue. I had lost all sense of time, and it didn't really matter. I had only one focus, and that was finding the next hit. I befriended some of the dealers. I would act like I was one of them, but I wasn't doing anything but fooling myself. I couldn't keep any money or drugs on me. I would trick with some of the young guys. It was kept quiet because they didn't want anyone to know they were buying sex, but in return I got the drugs. Their ages really didn't matter to me. If they were old enough to be out there hustling, they were old enough to trick with. I would find myself in various places, sometimes very strange places. I was on top of buildings, in hallways, in fields, and in bathrooms. I went wherever the drugs took me.

For some strange reason, I was extremely afraid of pimps, perhaps because I had heard stories from my oldest sister about what pimps do. I couldn't see lying on my back and working and then having to give my money to a man to control me. That was crazy, but so was what I was doing. But it was just a matter of time before I ran into a pimp, and I did. He didn't have a fur coat and high-heeled boots and a hat tilted to the side. He was a regular guy trying to talk fast, but what he didn't know was I had been out there long enough to learn the streets. I kept the conversation on the surface. I didn't give him too many details about myself. He said he could do this and that for me, but I was thinking I was doing fine by myself; it was nice talking to him, but no thanks. I knew that if I got hooked up with him that would be it for me. Crack cocaine was my pimp and the first opportunity I got, I literally ran. I do believe God kept me then too, because I know had I got hooked up with him that would have been the end for me. No one knew me or knew who I was or where I was from. I was basically Jane Doe. I had no identity other than the name they gave me, which was "Slim". That's all people really knew about me. At that time in my life, I was out there with no way to come back. I had a life sentence it seemed.

I came across an old lady, and, yes, she was out there getting high. Her name was Mrs. Johnson. She lived in Building 4 on the fourth floor of the projects. I believe she was terminally sick, but it didn't matter to me. That was her personal business. She said if I paid her, I could stay there, and because I was cute it made it easier for me to get the drugs. So I paid her in crack to stay there. She was fine with it. She had a lot of sons—it seemed like a house full—and on occasion I would sleep with one of them because most of them sold drugs. There was one who had a thing for me. He didn't want me doing what I was doing, so he would talk to me and let me stay in his room when he wasn't there.

He actually trusted me, and that was a big deal back then because I was so bad I couldn't trust myself.

I got threats from one guy who would rob me and take everything I had. One day I had enough. I told him I didn't have anything, and I ran. He actually chased me. I guess he knew, just as everybody else did, that I didn't belong there. I guess I was the only one who didn't know. He chased me straight to Mrs. Johnson's place. Thankfully, one of the guys who showed interest in me was there, and he jumped to defend me, even after the guy showed that he had a gun. I came to find out that Mrs. Johnson's boys were well known, and after realizing where I was and whom I was with, the guy backed off. After they had a few words, he left and never bothered me again. Who knows what was said, but from that point on, I knew it was no joke. Things were getting bad, and I was very close to danger—I felt it.

After hanging out a bit there, I heard a couple of the guys talking about having a house party. I was thinking, A house party? Who's the special guest going to be? No one could tell me I wasn't it, so I became very afraid. I could not show it, but the first chance I got I left and called Winston. I told him I was sorry for what I put him through, and that I was ready to go home. I asked if he could please come and pick me up, and he did. I knew in my heart that had I stayed and been at that house party, that would have been my end, and the feeling was so strong I could not ignore it. It was much more than paranoia.

Winston came for me and took me back home to my mom. I know he was relieved that I was off the street. But for some strange reason, I was not satisfied. I felt like I was missing something and I had to go back. So I fought a while with the thought and struggled to convince myself that I couldn't go back. I now know what was going on. I had been out there long enough to become addicted to the lifestyle, not just the drugs alone. It was all tied in together—the hustle, the edge, the danger. It was all a rush and something I had become so accustomed to that it became a part of my life, and I missed it. It's who I was, who I had become, anything else didn't feel like me. It felt like a part of me died, and I wasn't ready to say goodbye. This may sound strange, in fact, if I hadn't personally gone through these things, I would have thought all of it was made up, but that was my life on drugs.

After I returned home to my mom's, I was so tired. I wanted to do right, but I was still messed up mentally and emotionally. I was still trying to get it right by myself. I was still a mother and had to pull my life together so I could get my kids back and live a good life. As the days passed, I stayed in contact with Winston. He said he was going to be coming down with the boys. I was happy. I really did miss them. The night Winston said he was coming I was sitting outside on my mom's porch on Eleventh Street, waiting. I saw a little yellow car circling my area. I was still not altogether recovered or clean, but I was trying. I went over to the car, and the driver propositioned me. "Huh?" I thought, but before I even had time to process what was going on, I heard sirens as cars sped in to surround me. The driver of the yellow car was a vice cop. I don't even recall taking the proposition, things happened so fast. They arrested me and took me to jail.

I was thinking that I was only minutes from seeing my children. What was my mom going to say? I was really in jail. With all I had been through, I had never been in jail before. I was in the holding cell, and they called me out to book me and fingerprint me. It was all surreal. After the booking they said I had a choice. I could go to jail or I could give someone up. I don't know anybody, so who could you possibly want me to tell on? I thought. Immediately my mind started to race. I thought if I went ahead and cooperated, then I could go home, and Winston would never know I had been arrested for prostitution. I could just act like nothing ever happened, and then I could see my boys and try to get back on track. Therefore, I agreed to cooperate, not really knowing just what I had to do or who I had to give up. They called me back out, and as I was walking out of the holding cell, a lady said to me, "What they get you with?" I said prostitution, and she asked how many times I had been busted. I told her it was the first. She then said to me, "Oh, so that's why they are coming for you. But you don't have to do what they are asking you to do. It is your first offense; they have to let you go."

All I knew was I didn't want to be there. I had to get to my boys, and there was no way I could disappoint them again. I let what she said go in one ear and out the other. I was afraid and didn't know what to do. I couldn't call my mom, so I saw it as an opportunity to get out of jail fast and save face and the respect of my family. I couldn't have imagined that would be how I ended up, not me. I thought I was too cute for that, too smart for that, but the enemy was on me. I had opened up the door when I disobeyed my mother, and he saw that as an opportunity to get me, and he did; and the worst part is I allowed him to do it.

When the vice cop came to me and said the only way I could get out of jail was if I gave up someone, I couldn't think past my children and what my family was going to think or say about me; so rather than be patient and wait, because it looked like I was going to jail, I chose to cooperate when it was a lie. In actuality that was my first offense, and I could have gotten out on my own recognizance (ROR). So I agreed to do what they asked. I got out, and I was still able to see my children, and things were fine, or so I thought.

Then the police began to contact me. It seemed like they were actually following me. I would walk past street phones, and they would ring, and sure enough it was Brad, a vice cop, on the other end, telling me to meet him, and I would. A lot of the time, he would give me money to go to some random place and buy the drugs and give them back to the police. I saw it as just another hustle because as soon as he would give me the money, I would buy the drugs, but I also would pinch off of the rock and give him half of it, or I would bargain with the dealer to get more than the cop knew I was getting. So that became a hustle for me. I didn't want to snitch on anybody. I just wanted to use the drugs.

That went on for a little while, but then the relationship between Brad and me became a little more intense. I believe it was because he stopped seeing me as a drug addict and prostitute and began to see me as a real person, a woman. I began to find myself talking to him about personal things. He would even come to see me at my sister Liana's house. I didn't know what his motives were then, but I believe they were for more than just work purposes. Our conversation got so heated at one point that it was like a television show or a movie or something. I think we both forgot who we were and what we were doing. All I can remember is we were rather close. I had been attracted to him for some time, and we were standing close in my sister's living room, and one of the guys from upstairs came down and knocked on the door and said, "Can I have a nickel?" Come to find out, my sister was smoking weed for pleasure, and the guy from upstairs wanted some and while Brad was standing there, he asked for some weed. Brad's response was, "I'm not on the clock," and that was the last I heard about that. We laughed it off. My sister took her little weed can and headed upstairs, leaving Brad and me downstairs in the living room. We went back to talking while standing in my sister's living room, and all of a sudden out of nowhere we got closer and closer to each other until our eyes were locked and fixed on each other. Then it happened. He leaned in, and I gave in. We began to kiss ever so passionately, like we were living in a totally different world than the one we were in. Then the door opened. It was Liana. I thought if she had waited just a few minutes, who knows what might have happened? My self-esteem had been torn to shreds, and I just didn't feel worthy to be wanted, so when that cop took an interest in me, it was a huge boost. It felt good to be wanted again. But after the door opened, reality set back in, and that moment was gone forever, never to return again. After that I heard less from him. I went out again and forgot all about what I agreed to do for the police. They forgot too, so I left it at that—or maybe they didn't forget, maybe Brad put in a good word for me or they just simply figured out they were wasting their time with me.

My court date came up, and Brad was supposed to put in a good word for me. Because it was my first offense, I got one-year probation. The probation was like a Band-Aid. It just covered my problem for a little while, but it didn't fix it. As soon as I got tired of all the programs and urine samples and just stopped caring, I was out there again, and sure enough after giving a dirty urine sample, they locked me back up. That time things were different. They took me to another part of the jail, past the holding cell area. I had bail, but my mom wasn't about to pay it. I believe she felt better knowing where I was and that I was safe. I was on a path of destruction, almost like a runaway train with no breaks, and the only thing that could slow me down without killing me was jail.

CHAPTER 12

The Lion and the Prey

We're never so vulnerable than when we trust someone - but paradoxically, if we cannot trust, neither can we find love or joy. ~ Walter Anderson

B eing in jail did slow me down. I had nowhere else to go, and lots of time on my hands. It was actually the place where I got an understanding of God through Jesus Christ. I grew up in churches, but in jail I read the whole book of Psalms and the whole book of Proverbs, for the first time and that is where I learned how I should be living. Everything became different. Things that I found myself doing that were wrong became magnified. I became aware of it and wanted to do better. Some of the women in there weren't too pleasant, and I found myself wanting to fight, but I didn't. Instead, I would just go back to my cell and cry. I didn't understand what was going on, but I now know it was a transformation taking place in me. Though I hadn't gotten clean yet, I was ready to receive conviction and direction from the Holy Spirit without even realizing that was what was going on. Before that, I would have just fought, but now I was beginning to learn how to humble myself.

I didn't mysteriously get clean overnight. In fact, my journey with drug addiction was still far from over. When I got out, I still ended up back in the streets, but I was different. I didn't want to steal from anybody. I became more consciously aware of what I was doing, even when I was doing wrong. Before that, I didn't even have a conscience. I found myself smiling so much that a drug dealer would ask me all the time why I was always smiling even when I was trying to hustle him, and my response was, "I don't know. I just feel like smiling." Now I know why. I had the joy of the Lord even in the valley of the shadow of death.

Things began to change and with change came growth, and because of that growth, I was now open to the idea of actually wanting to be clean and sober. I knew I needed to get myself together for my children, and I knew my family loved me, and I wondered why I was hurting myself and them like that. But most of all I had a desire to do it for myself so that I could please God. But I still ignored those thoughts and stayed out there a while longer. Then one-day things got so bad and I had been out so long, I realized I was hungry and tired of running, and all I wanted was water. I was at a crack house where people would get high, and the morning light was coming through the window. I asked the lady of the house for water. I was sitting in her living room, and she came back with the water in a cup, but she was giggling. She gave me the water and then quickly went into her bedroom, where another girl was. I could hear her giggling and whispering and as I started to take a gulp of water, it dawned on me that the woman had spit in the cup and given it to me to drink. I immediately spit the water back into the cup, ran to the kitchen, threw the cup in the sink, and put my mouth to the faucet and drank until my belly was full then I left. That is where my trust issues with people bringing me food or drink came from. I have to see the drink come from a closed bottle or the food prepared. I believe that is where the obsessive-compulsive behavior came from as well, because for a while I couldn't eat ketchup from a restaurant unless it came from packets. I was constantly washing my hands. Even before I stepped out of the shower, I had to wash my hands. That little stunt messed me up badly, so I became one of the cleanest drug addicts out there. I used to walk around with my toothbrush in my back pocket, and I constantly had to bathe. I can recall taking baths in many strange bathrooms. I had to be clean; after all, look at the lifestyle I was living. I didn't realize the whole time that while I was trying to get the outside cleansed, my internal spirit was begging for a cleaning as well.

I was still on probation, and I wasn't checking in. I was just missing in action for a while. Then I showed up at my mom's house. I was tired and ready to sleep, and I knew I would be safe at my mom's house. I could sleep without being bothered. But my mom's philosophy was if you are not going to clean up on your own, I'm going to help you get clean and sober. So she called my probation officer. When I woke up, I woke up to some strange, tall white man with his hair in a ponytail, saying, "Miss Vereen, it's time to get up." When I realized what was going on, it was already too late. I began to cry and asked her, why she was doing that to me? Why did she hate me? I knew she was doing it because she loved me, but in the moment I felt betrayed. In her eyes I was that same little, chubby girl she raised to be full of love. I was her baby, and the drugs had stolen me away from her. She wanted me back, and what she did on that day was the best thing she could have done for me. I believe she saved my life.

They took me to jail and put me in the main jail population. After I slept, showered, and ate, I began to wonder, how on earth did I end up back in jail again? As I reflected, it came to me that I was there because of the choices and decisions I made. There was a good side to the predicament I put myself in, but I was still bound by the drugs, and in order to clean up and fix the problem, I had to go through it, take it head on, and fight to get back where I needed to be. That was my new objective. If I wanted to live, I had to fight for my life, and that's what I did from that point on. Everything didn't become perfect magically; it was a fight and not just a battle but also a war.

As I was there, trying to get my mind right, I saw a corrections officer. He was tall. I didn't even know if he was cute or not, but he had begun to show me some interest. I couldn't imagine that he wanted me. I was feeling low, unattractive, and just hurt and beat down. I soon found out it wasn't just in my head because he began to write me letters through the mail. It was all so strange, but it was exciting. I just couldn't fathom the idea that a corrections officer, someone of authority, wanted me, but he did. He began to come to our pod more frequently; and when he was assigned to watch over us, he would stare at me. It should have been creepy, but I began to feel butterflies when he would show up, I was so excited. After all, there wasn't much else to do in jail. It was the same old routine day in and day out. The whole experience brought some excitement to my life, so I went with it and I would stare back at him. In my sick mind, he was my man. I didn't even know if he was married or not. I didn't even think about it, to be honest. He was coming to see about me, inquiring about me, and how I was doing.

Then on a normal night, lights were out and the pod was quiet, so quiet you could hear a pin drop. I was sleeping when all of a sudden I felt a tap on my shoulder. I didn't understand it because I had my own cell. When I opened my eyes, I saw him, Officer Banks, hovering over me. I was nervous, and confused, then he whispered to me to come downstairs and meet him in the library on the pod. Everyone was sleeping, and I started to feel a surge of exhilaration. My adrenaline was pumping, there was so much risk, but I tiptoed straight downstairs in disbelief of what was happening. When I got to the library, he began to kiss me passionately and feel me up. We had a bit of conversation then more kissing and fondling. Then after a bit of foreplay, he instructed me to go back up to my cell. I was feeling like I was on top of the world. There I was, a little strung-out crack addict in jail, on a probation violation for prostitution, and a correctional officer, who was clean-cut, had a good job, and appeared to be a model citizen, wanted me. I was in disbelief, but nevertheless I felt great and yet so very vulnerable, and he played on that.

I got a letter in the mail a couple days later, and that letter was very strange. It said some personal things about him, how he didn't have any hair on his body, how he shaved everywhere, and how he wanted to have sex with me with a butt plug. I didn't even know what a butt plug was. I had to ask some of the other women in there what it was. He talked about fishing and some other things, and at the bottom of the letter, he instructed me to destroy the letters each time I got them. But I did not. Instead, I kept them for my own belief, my own satisfaction, and my own proof. I never intended for anyone to see any of the letters, or read them. After all, I believed that he was my guy. I was so naïve, young, dumb, and stupid, and on top of that I was still an addict with no sense of direction. All I ever wanted was love, and I guess I didn't care where it came from.

The next time he had to work our pod at night, he unlocked my cell door remotely, lights were out, and it was after midnight. The pod was silent. There was no movement. All of a sudden, I woke up to the sound of my cell door opening. I wondered what was going on, and I stuck my head out to see him. That time he gestured for me to come down and meet him in the library. Without hesitation I went. I tiptoed down the stairs, and there he was. Immediately, he took me into his arms and began to kiss me. Then he turned me around and began to perform oral sex on me, and then it happened. He and I had sex. There were no condoms used, nor did he or I give it a second thought, things were moving so fast. When it was over, he told me not to tell, and he would see me again. I went back up to my cell and just laid there thinking that I must be dreaming or in a movie or something, it was so surreal.

The next morning I was running around on cloud nine, just in deep thought about what had happened. I guess I was happy and high, not from drugs, but the intense attention he showed me resulting in a forbidden sexual act, and it made me feel good. A few days went by, and then I saw the white shirt sergeants and other officers go straight upstairs. When they first came through the pod, everyone was wondering what was going on. Then they made their way up to my cell and shook the whole thing down. I was wondering what they were doing and why they were in my cell. Now at times they did do random searches, but I knew I hadn't given them a reason to suspect me of anything. They searched everything and found just what they were looking for and what they needed to nail Officer Banks.

I found out a couple of the girls were gossiping about him and me and his behavior toward me, and most likely when I thought everyone was sleeping those two nights, perhaps not everyone was sleeping. Then another girl came up to me asking questions, and I didn't understand why. I came to find out he was sleeping with her also. She was known for having seizures. She was sick with epilepsy, but he was having sex with her too.

I was furious. He had betrayed me, cheated on me, and put me at risk. I really thought I had a reason to be upset and angry with him because he was sleeping with another inmate. She did in fact have a couple of quiet nights with him too, but she told. That is how everything came out. I'm not sure what her motives were, but I began to understand why he wanted me to get rid of the letters. He didn't want there to be any evidence. But I had the smoking gun, and they found it. Ironically, the day I was scheduled for release was the day the warden questioned me about the whole situation. He told me the officer said the girl was lying, and I knew I didn't say anything, but he was calling me a liar too, so they obviously questioned him about me. They had the proof. I didn't really have to expose him; he did that all on his own. There were questions, and I admitted to sleeping with him but also expressed that I didn't want to get him into any trouble. I wanted to protect him from losing all that he worked so hard for. I didn't want to be the cause of his life being torn inside out, but it couldn't be prevented or stopped.

The warden asked if I would be willing to tell what happened, and I agreed to do that. After all, he called me a liar and tried to make me look worse than I already felt about the whole situation. I felt dirty, like I had been raped or molested although it was consensual. He made me sound like the crack addict I was, like I was worthless. And maybe at that time I did look bad and didn't appear to be worth much, but he still chose to sleep with me, unprotected no less, so it didn't really say much for him either.

When the time came, there was a little hearing, and he was found guilty. He lost his job, his pension, his retirement, and his dignity—talk about humility. He was on top for some time, taking advantage of us sick addicts who didn't know better, but he ended up losing everything.

CHAPTER 13

Love, Marriage and Addiction

Wives, submit to your husbands, as is fitting in the Lord. Husbands, love your wives and do not be harsh with them. ~ Colossians 3:18-19

Shortly after, I was released and I went to stay with my mom again. I did continue to try to get clean. I was doing well, and I stayed clean for a while. One day I asked my mom if it was okay to walk over to the Hamilton Mall. Hamilton was not like one of the big malls with all the stores inside. It was simply a strip mall of stores. My mother lived on Eleventh Street in Allentown, and the mall was on Ninth Street. I wanted to get some air, and I wanted to go to the post office to drop off a letter. I had a boyfriend named Black, whom I had met in jail, and I had written him a letter and wanted to mail it to him. The post office was among the stores at the end of the mall. I actually asked my mom's permission to go. I was trying to do everything right. I didn't want to disappoint her or go back to jail. I was walking a straight line.

I was on my way to the post office, when I saw a dark-skinned man. He had a sexy swagger to him and he walked with confidence. He was clean-cut and was wearing black jeans, blue-and-black sneakers, and a black shirt with blue stripes coming down the shirt. Across the bottom of the shirt, the word BOSS was written. He looked so handsome to me. He was one of the first guys I saw in a long time that appeared to be normal, drug-free, and just a regular kind of guy. After he walked by me, I took about four more steps and then turned and looked back. He had already crossed the street, and just as I looked back, so did he. I knew that was my chance to break the ice. He looked at me, and I gestured for him to come back, and he did. He actually thought I was my sister. I let him know I wasn't and that we were triplets. We looked alike, but we were very different. He said he had known Liana from the Jamaican club and said we looked so much alike. That was the ice-breaking moment to talk to him. He told me his name was Michael, and we exchanged phone numbers. When I got back from the post office, I called him, and we talked more. I found out that he was

Jamaican and he was only three years older than me. We had a lot in common and made an instant connection.

Michael then started to come around to my mom's house to visit me. Things seemed fine. I was in a program as a requirement of the probation/parole I was on. Michael started coming by my mom's house early in the morning and walking me to the day program, which was on Linden Street, a block or two away. When the session was over, he would be there, waiting to walk me back to my mom's house. I thought he was so sweet, and every time I saw him he was well dressed and very appealing. He and I then began an intimate relationship. Things were going so well I had forgotten all about my little boyfriend Black, who was in jail. I had a real man, who wanted me, and we were compatible. He had no idea of my drug addiction. As far as I was concerned, all that was over. It was time for me to start everything fresh and move forward. I just knew my past was going to go away, and he wouldn't find out—at least not everything—because I wasn't going to tell him. All he knew was that I had been in jail for something stupid and I had to go to the program to satisfy the terms of the probation. He was okay with that.

When we began to get close, he was coming to see me every day and when we weren't together, I would write him love letters. I honestly felt like a love-struck teenage girl. It was something I hadn't really experienced before that was actually real and didn't change part way into the relationship. Due to the fact that I had started the drugs at such an early age, my mind wasn't developed past a certain point. I was still a child in many ways, still a bit immature. I had no responsibilities. My children were all being taken care of. All I had to do was work on me, and I was trying. Michael and I got better acquainted. We were now boyfriend and girlfriend. I was feeling really good, knowing that after all I had been through, there was a man who was attracted to me, who wanted me, and who was there for me. He became my world.

Two months went by, and I started to hear talk of marriage. That sounded wonderful to me. I wanted to settle down, change my life, get my kids back, and provide for them, and with Michael I saw the opportunity to do it. One day Michael came over and asked me, "Will you marry me?" I thought it was cute, and he put a ring on my finger. It wasn't a real diamond, but it was mine, and I knew he did the best he could. All I saw was love. He put love around my finger and sealed it with a kiss. Immediately, I said yes.

My mom got me a job at Burger King, which was also her second job. I was doing great. I was pulling my life back together by God's good grace. I had a job, I had a man I was about to marry, and we were working on getting our first apartment. My mom was renting an apartment from Mr. Kross, the same man who rented me the apartment across from Carlito's Bar and Grill next to the graveyard years earlier. He had evicted me from that apartment, but times had changed, and things were different now. I had my mom talk to him about renting me an apartment. My sister Buffy had been renting the apartment my mom used to rent from Jonathan in the old building on North Seventh Street. When my mom left, Buffy had simply taken over the lease. Understandably, Jonathan had some concerns, but my mom told him I was about to get married, I had good references from work, and there was a vacant apartment up from Buffy's apartment on the third floor. I told my Mom that apartment would be fine without even thinking about it. I felt I was ready to move forward and be responsible. So Jonathan told my mom he would rent the third-floor apartment to us. All we needed was the first month's rent and a deposit, which was equivalent to the rent. I told Michael about it, and he came up with a small portion to contribute. I came up with the rest. I didn't mind because I knew I could get the money. I began to work double shifts and take other workers' hours. I closed a few nights of the week. So I got the money, and I worked for it. I was still clean and concentrating on building our family and future together as well as becoming responsible.

Michael was there for me, and little by little I began to tell him the whole story of my life. He still didn't judge me, but I don't think he really believed me. Finally, we got the keys after coming up with all the money. All we had was a comforter, but little by little we worked our way up to a mattress and then a bed and then a table for the kitchen. We literally started from the bottom and worked our way up. The bright side to being at the bottom was it was easy to see which direction to go and that was up. After a while Michael got a job and would get up early morning hours to go to work, things seemed to be normal. Then we started talking about getting my kids back and providing for them a good and secure home and just being a family for them. After all, I had put them through enough. It was time to be the good mother and effective parent they needed. I had never been married before, so I didn't know much about it, but I was trying to be a good wife as well. Michael was good to me. I could talk to him, and he was great for the kids.

After doing an extensive review of our lives, we decided to try to get the kids back. We both were doing everything right. Winston then began to bring the boys for visits, and Lilly and Georgia, Lilly's niece, made it easy for me to get the boys until finally I was ready to keep them. Georgia had offered to also take care of my youngest son Daquan; he was my fifth child at that time. I worked hard and stayed clean. Things were fine, and Michael backed me 100 percent. He was truly there for me, and he was an awesome dad. I didn't always understand where he was getting most of the things from, but he did provide for a while, so life was good. I got all four of my boys back. Laquan stayed with my mother. It was a fight, but we did what we had to do. We stuck together, and things were working out, and I was happy. When I had to work, Michael stayed home with the kids. They were all young back then, but Michael was good with them.

I kept requesting more hours, and I was happy with it for a while. Then I asked to transfer to the Burger King that was closer to our apartment. I thought that would be a better location, and my cousin worked there as a manager; I figured I would get more hours. To my shock and amazement, I got the transfer to the Burger King on MacArthur Road in Allentown, up from Seventh Street and close by our apartment. Things were going in my favor and I was feeling very positive about the future. I was working and with my family. But then I started noticing things about my cousin that were strange. He began to miss work and went to the bathroom often. Then one day I went to the bathroom to clean and I found a bag of heroin. I was shocked and I questioned him, and he said he was holding it for someone. I dismissed it then, but things were still unusual. His behavior was very suspicious and familiar. I had been around a lot of heroin users, so I suspected him despite his excuses. I became increasingly concerned, and I think I let it affect me way more than it should have. That was his life, and I had my own addictions and demons that I was trying to suppress.

Then one day in a slurred voice he said he needed to leave and that he had just thrown up. Sure enough my suspicions were confirmed.

He was using heroin while on the job. I had never been able to understand how some people can use drugs and hold down a job. I guess it is very rare because it seems to always catch up to them. My cousin started missing days from work. His whole life began spiraling downhill, and I was there watching it, subconsciously thinking that all it would take to ruin my life was one hit. Then everything I worked so hard for would go down the drain.

They soon fired my cousin and that was when things in my mind began to go haywire. Being in such close proximity to drugs, finding it in the restroom at work, touching it, and the thoughts of my cousin using, made me get small cravings and urges. The problem was that I didn't dismiss the thoughts. I held on to them thinking they were harmless and innocent, and I kept these thoughts secret. When I got my very next paycheck, I remember being afraid because the thoughts started to take over my mind. I began to tell myself I could just get one bag and that would satisfy me. I had the money, and the whole time I was having these thoughts, I never once thought to just express them and reveal them so I could really deal with them. The truth is, I hadn't decided whether or not I was going to give in or fight another day. Instead, I began to convince myself if I used just one more time, I would never do it again.

Sadly, thoughts eventually become actions, and actions become habits. I got my money and disappeared for a few hours and allowed my addiction to take over. I went with it, and all I did was pick right up where I had left off before going to jail. I didn't stop using until all the money was gone. I could not believe what I did. I was afraid to go back home, but I did. Michael and I cried together because I was truly sorry for letting him down. I had come so far and even gotten the kids back. For me to relapse was unbelievable, but I allowed it to consume me in such a way that I just couldn't stop.

More and more I began to make excuses for wanting to be out there. I began to miss so many days at work that I quit. I was really going at it, back on drugs, but in a more hidden way. Because Michael was helping me hide it, he felt ashamed. At first, I did too, until the addiction spun out of control. We were not even married yet and we had all the kids back, and I was messing up. The guilt only made it worse. I had gone backward so much that I was getting high with a girl I used to get high with previously; she lived directly across the street from us. Michael didn't even know where I was, but I was right across the street from our apartment, sitting in there getting high.

I used so much and so quickly that I got paranoid beyond belief. I got so paranoid I forgot where the door was. But I had to get out of her apartment, so I decided to go out the window, which was a story up. I couldn't understand why these people were trying to hold me hostage while I was trying to escape through the window. My mind told me they were going to hurt me and that I had to get out of that apartment by any means necessary, so out the window I went. I had tucked my money into my shoes for fear they were going to try to rob me. My friend and a big guy were there in her apartment, and what made me so scared was that her guy friend started talking about her and me getting it on. I was thinking, that I bought those drugs. I didn't have to trick or freak for those. I had money. In fact, it was my money that financed that little crack party. I was fighting to get out the window because I could not take the paranoia any more. As I struggled, my shoes came off, so they got the money.

As I was half hanging out the window, all of a sudden I saw Michael come running up, so I must have been screaming for him. I was deathly afraid, and no one was going to stop me from getting out that window. My mom was at my sister's house that morning, and my sister and my mom came running over to see what was going on. I was so embarrassed and ashamed when I came down off that high, but at the time that was just another reaction to smoking crack, and things only got worse. As I squirmed out the window, people were pulling me from up top, and some were at the bottom waiting to catch me. For just a moment I thought, "Look at what I'm doing to myself." But my thoughts quickly turned back to getting to safety, and safety for me was out of that apartment.

We were just days from our wedding, and look at what I was doing. I disappointed my mother and myself. Michael was ashamed too. I could see it on his face. But he never left. In fact, we got married on August 23, 1997. I was still so messed up, but we went through with the wedding, and for a very brief time things were normal. I stopped using for a couple days, and we let go of what had occurred. I promised not to do it again, and the whole focus was on our getting married.

There were some who said we were rushing things, and others who said it was just so he could get his green card because he was from Jamaica and here in America illegally. But my heart said it was for love, and that is what he showed me, unconditional love.

We thought if we went ahead with the wedding it would fix things, but it did not. I really didn't know how to be a mother, let alone a wife. My husband came along and taught me a lot. Even though I thought I already knew everything, I had no clue. I thought I was going to be able to get married and still do the things I was doing. I didn't even think about growth, change, or commitment. When we got married I had only known my husband for six months, I was 24 with 5 children and I was just sort of going with the flow. My mind was still on the streets.

However, I desperately tried everything to change, or so I thought. I gave marriage a try. It was something new. I had never experienced it and wanted to know what it was like. Was it going to be like what I saw on television, with a happy ending? Was it going to be easy? Was it going to make me change and be better overnight? It was none of the above.

The only difference between then and my previous time on the street was that I was married and living in an apartment, and I didn't have to trick for the drugs. Somehow I had the money for drugs, or maybe it was just that when I had money, I took advantage of the situation. As soon as the money touched my hand or I knew I was getting money, the next thought became the drugs. When there was no money in my hands, I was a completely different woman; I was the mother, wife, and person I needed to be. But as soon as the money hit my hand, my belly began to turn and twist, I began to get the butterflies, and then I began to feel like I had to go to the bathroom to release my bowels. That happened every single time.

God sent me a man who stood by me through thick and thin, no matter what people would say. We went through lots of hard times, but when I didn't have any money the times were the best. We watched movies together with the kids, and we ate ice cream. Sex was even nice. We spent all our time together. I was not proud of it, but at the time I was still consumed by the addiction. Confusion had overtaken me. I was torn between the life of a mother and wife and that of a crack addict. That was not fun because I knew what I needed to be doing, and

I knew what I wanted to be doing, but that was all different from what I actually did. I am so grateful for Michael. He held us together until I was able to do it.

CHAPTER 14

Knowledge and Awareness

It takes courage...to endure the sharp pains of self discovery rather than choose to take the dull pain of unconsciousness that would last the rest of our lives. - Marianne Williamson

I was still using occasionally, but I had begun to fight for my life once again. I inquired about my GED because I had dropped out of school in the tenth grade and had a baby, and since then had four more. I was 26, I didn't have a high school diploma, and I started thinking about my future. A future without drugs couldn't happen without proper planning and something to look forward to. Something to work toward, I realized I needed some kind of an education for a better future. At the time I thought I was living on top of the world, but I wasn't fooling anyone but myself. After learning what I needed to do to get my GED, I did exactly that. I got my GED, and for the first time, I had a different kind of high. Accomplishment was an amazing feeling, and I wanted more. Shortly after getting my GED, I inquired about taking classes at Lehigh Carbon Community College. I did it immediately because I knew if I didn't, I would get lazy, and I really wanted to do something with my life, so I enrolled in college. I had to do what I could to keep my mind occupied.

I still had a monkey on my back, riding me like I owed it something. My intentions were great. I wanted to change, and I took the steps to change, but it was still a fight. The crack knew my name well, and at times it screamed and yelled for me, "Ivana! Ivana!" That's when I realized I wasn't in a battle; it was a full-fledged war for my future, and for my soul.

When it came time for me to start my classes, I wanted at first to major in social sciences. I really wanted to work with people and learn how they think and what makes them behave the way they do. I wanted to figure out what causes some people to become addicts. I thought for sure that was the field for me. I guess I wanted to figure out what causes people like me to become addicts. I thought school was going to keep me clean because I had a plan and set some goals for myself. I found out quickly that school was not a cure, just a good distraction. It took some more falls and fights for me to realize I had the power to stop me; I just had to want to.

Those first and second semesters were not easy, but I did great. I had the major I thought I really wanted, and I took all the classes I was most comfortable with. Things were going great. I was going to classes faithfully, and I felt like I really belonged. When I was on the school campus, I felt like I was just one of the students. No one had any idea I was a crack addict. All others saw was another college student trying to better herself. I participated in all my classes; and if you asked me, I would say I made it exciting because I wanted to know everything. I guess you can say I kept the classes going with all my questions. The interaction with my classmates and professors was awesome, and I fit right in with the rest of them.

Then came the third semester, and all the money for grants, loans and books. Sure enough, when I had that money in my hand, there went my bowels and my stomach rumbling. My hands got sweaty, and the anxiety began to set in. That monkey began to scream at me, saying, "Ivana, you know very well what we have to do to get these symptoms to cease." I listened. I gave in, and as soon as I could and as quickly as I could, I was on my way to Allentown to buy some crack. I totally lived for that drug, and it is only through the grace of God that I didn't die from it. I knew I was doing too much, but the more I had, the more I wanted. It was a vicious cycle. There were many times that I smoked up the rent money, food money, clothes money, and bill money. When all the money was gone and I showered and slept, I was back to being the student, mom and wife. Things appeared to be fine, but they weren't. I just could not handle money. For a long time, I had to give the money I would get from public assistance to Michael because I didn't trust myself. I wanted to do right, and I kept fighting. There were more slips and more falls, but I didn't stop going to school.

I grew so tired of disappointing my children, and my husband, but also tired of hurting myself; I just wanted it to stop. I became much more focused on school. Michael helped me with the money I was receiving so I wouldn't continue to mess up. I began to desire a closer relationship with God and I was finally ready to quit. God gave me the strength to walk away and the desire to be freed from the bondage of crack cocaine. It was in the year 2001 that I took my last hit of crack cocaine. It was then that I received my deliverance and new way of life. We were living in Slatington, Pennsylvania and I was finally crack-free. I graduated in 2006 with my degree in criminal justice, but I had a ways to go. After the drugs I picked up the clubs and drinking so in actuality all I did was trade in one addiction for the next.

I minimized the consumption of my drinking and made excuses because it wasn't my drug of choice. When I was released from the drugs, my deliverance had really just begun. I found myself struggling with others things trying so desperately to fill the void that the cocaine once inhabited. I was truly in prison, a prisoner to the drugs, and a prison in my mind, even a prisoner to the lies I told myself to make being drunk in the clubs okay. My mind was still so very polluted and filled with darkness. Only the light of Christ could clear up the fog that consumed my mind with false pride and illusions that made everything look normal. I tried but I still had a long way to go.

With the crack habit behind me, I totally transformed into a so-called hot girl. My triplet sister and I would drive to Philadelphia and New York to go party because nobody there would recognize me for the crack addict I once was. When we went out, I would go in the latest fashions. My husband hustled clothes so I had new everything, and before I knew it smoking crack was a distant memory. I was done with crack, but I was far from fixed. My mind was still messed up. I was paranoid to the point that I started having anxiety attacks. That was very embarrassing to me. How could I be a hot girl while having anxiety attacks? As soon as the club got crowded, here came that feeling of having to use the bathroom and heavy breathing like I was about to pass out. How could that be cute for a self-proclaimed hot girl that all the men wanted?

My sister and I were known as the Black Diamond Ladies, a little crew known for the latest dances, stylish clothes, heavy jewelry, different cars, and just being really well maintained. That was funny because there were times that when we got to the club, all we had was money enough for the first couple of drinks and gas money to get back home, and that was it. Most of the time, because we looked good, guys would buy us drinks. We enjoyed ourselves. We thought we were living on top of the world.

When we started building our name and becoming known, that did us some good. Simply because of who we were, they let us into the clubs free. At some of the clubs we frequented, we were soon greeting others with hugs and receiving hugs. We simply walked past the security checkpoint and the window or door, if payment was required, and then headed straight for the bathroom to check our appearance. Later, after we got past the introductions and protocol, we didn't even bother to stop. We were the celebrities, and nobody could tell us we weren't. We walked with confidence with our heads looking forward and with a strut that was out of that world. We could feel everyone in the club looking at us, and that only gave us more confidence. Then after getting our drinks, we went to where we wanted to stand in the club, which was usually wherever the DJ was; or if there was a stage, we were there. We scanned the place, and if people we knew from the club were in our immediate path, we would give hugs; otherwise, it was straight to the center, where we got the most attention. That became my new addiction.

Over the course of the years, I became an extremist. Everything I did was to the extreme. When I sought the crack, I went all out and was not going to leave wherever I was until I got it and used it all up. When I dressed to go to the clubs, I had to be in the best and most revealing sexy clothes. I had to get the most attention. And then, when I drank, I had to drink until I didn't want any more. It was never because I was unable to get it, because I always got it. We befriended a few bar owners for that reason. We loved the power that came along with the friendships. But after a while that innocent friendship was not enough for the guys, and we found other bars. I figured I had already been through the whole sex thing, and after looking back at how God had spared my life and saved me, there was no way I was going to be out there sleeping with men just for attention or a drink. I had come too far for that. They didn't know anything about my past, and I used that to the fullest in my nightlife. I was just another Black Diamond Lady.

The sad part is that I would express to Michael my feeling that things would be better if we did more things together more often. I would say to him, "If you want our relationship to work, you have to show me more attention, because the guys out there in the clubs are giving me the attention, and I like it." He just didn't seem to get it.

I was beginning to think he was ashamed of me. He never went to the clubs with us; he would just let me go, knowing I wasn't coming in until the next morning. He was fine with it, but deep down I wasn't. All I wanted was love—to feel love, to be loved, and to be in love, but I wasn't sure what love looked or felt like. So I began to look for it. It turned out what I did find was lust, not real love at all, and a couple of times after I got tired of it; I stopped seeing the guy that would make me feel loved. It wasn't the guy that would stop seeing me; I was a Black Diamond Lady, and I had to keep up a certain appearance and image to support the reputation I built for the club, which wasn't bad. After a few drinks, I became a lot more flirtatious, but nobody could talk to me in a disrespectful manner. I didn't allow it. I didn't have to because we were known as the dancers in the party.

One particular night I was out with Gloria, one of our associates we sometimes hung out with. That night Liana wasn't with me. That was bad because if my sister wasn't there, it was like I was lost and made horrible decisions. I met a guy in the club who said he had been watching us for a while in the reggae clubs, and he noticed I didn't talk to just anybody. He wanted to know who I was. I couldn't be seen talking to just anybody because of our image, but at the same time I didn't want to act like I was better than everybody else or stuck up, so I talked to him. He was cute, and I was drunk, which is not a very good combination. In fact, it was a dangerous mix. However, we danced and got to know each other, but there wasn't much to it.

Gloria hooked up with a guy, and I was with the guy I had been dancing with. He suggested we go to his friend's house, and I did something I had never done. I told Gloria I would meet up with her later. I guess I really didn't think things through, because in hindsight it was pretty clear what was going to happen at 4:00 a.m. after we had both been drinking. We went to his friend's house, and sure enough he wanted sex. I looked at him like he was crazy and told him that I was not having sex on nobody's floor. The least he could do is take me to a hotel. The buzz was wearing off, I was getting tired, and I did want to get some sleep. So the guy finally found a hotel that had vacancies. He had given me money earlier for drinks, which I didn't spend because I had enough. I did have a limit, and that was the point just before vomiting. I just wanted to sleep because I was so tired. After getting the room, we still had our clothes on and there was some activity going on. He was anxious, though, and I went with it. He put on a condom, and before I knew it, it was over. He suggested for me to go take a shower. I did, and when I came out, he was gone. Something told me to go check my purse. The money he had given me was gone too. I was stranded in a hotel room in Philly with no money or transportation to get home. Thank God Gloria was still in Philly. I went to the front desk to see if maybe he was out there, but he and his car were gone. I asked when checkout time was, and the guy at the front desk told me 11:00 a.m. I called Gloria and I was so relieved that she was still in the area. She didn't leave me. Before checkout she came and got me.

I had gone through some embarrassing things in my life, but was I ever ashamed now. I thought I was a celebrity who commanded respect. But he brought me to a hotel, took back the money he had given me, and left me; and I didn't even know his full name. That was what alcohol and living the nightlife did to me. I knew better than to go out without my sister. When she was there, things like that never happened. We were a force when we were together, and things people could get over on one of us they could never get over on the two of us together. I thank God for my sister Liana. Yes, it was very degrading, embarrassing and shameful but it did happen. The shame was overwhelming, but that was something I had to get through to get to my next level.

Often times by the time I got home Michael would be on the couch. I loved him and wanted our marriage to work, but I don't think he wanted me. I guess it was because of the nightlife and the things I was doing. He knew about all of it because I told him.

My conscience wouldn't let me keep any secrets. I had to tell him and try to be honest with him. I thought it was only fair and that telling him about my activities would change things somehow and he would finally come around and see what we could do to fix the situations I often created. But after the forgiveness, things only stayed the same, and then our arguments got worse. Still he stayed, but because there was no change, the forgiveness turned to disgust and hate. Maybe he stayed because of the kids, his citizenship or me, but he needed to change as well because I took full advantage of the fact that I was paying all the bills. I thought that allowed me to do whatever I wanted, and after a while I wanted a regular husband I could love and would show me that he loved me too. There were things sexually he didn't want to explore with me, so I went out and found it. It was very unhealthy, but he just wouldn't understand. Things went from bad to worse. I found myself looking for other relationships while I was married. There were a couple of men I really fell for, but because I had been with Michael so long I was afraid to pursue them. I stayed even though we were both miserable.

When I went back to the clubs, I tried even harder to maintain my image. I didn't talk to any guys like that again, unless they were equally suited for me. People continued to love my sister and me, and no one ever found out what happened. We continued to greet people with love and hugs. The people loved us because we were full of love. If we began talking to someone, whether a guy or a girl, before we left the conversation, we gave hugs; and the next time we saw that person, it was like we were instant club associates. We weren't too big on friends per se. I was my sister's friend, and she was mine. Other people were associates. We had a few other girls who were close to us, but for the most part it was just Liana and I. We were known best for giving hugs. Even when we met celebrities, we embraced them the same way; and when we saw them again, we gave them hugs again like they were old friends. As such, we became celebrity associates, and in the eyes of a lot of club-goers, we were working our way up. But I was still so lonely I felt like I was single even while married. I began to live as if I didn't have a husband but only a roommate. I wanted more attention, but because I was always going out looking for it, Michael refused to give me attention. I didn't know how to fix it and didn't even know if I wanted to fix the situation. I just wanted to be loved for who I was, not just for what I could give or do.

CHAPTER 15

Sin Cycles: Wash, Rinse, Repeat

O wretched man that I am! Who will deliver me from this body of death?. ~ Romans 7:24

In 2002, I was 29 and pregnant with my seventh child, my daughter Princess. My other six children were all boys. I always wanted a little girl and I finally got her; it only took seven times. Through all my pregnancies, I never once gave any thought to how many kids I was having or wanted to have. What was going through my mind was that I was pregnant and I had to take care of them despite the condition I was in. That was pretty much it. The best part of loving a child is that regardless of anything, they love you back. So when the man left, I still had my babies, no matter how messed up I was I knew I had to take care of my babies.

I had been clean for a couple of years at that point. My mom had been battling breast cancer, and we moved from Slatington to be closer to her. Just before I gave birth to my daughter Princess on March 10, 2002, my mom, my best friend, and the rock of our family, passed away. That was a hard time for us. We had just moved back to Allentown and were trying to fix things with our marriage and at the same time be there for my mom. We watched her as she fought to breathe and to walk. That was hard, but praise God, she didn't suffer long, and I do believe in my heart she went when God was ready for her, she did her job.

I wasn't totally right, but I was no longer on crack cocaine and barely smoking weed. We were living on Carrot Street in Allentown. I had become responsible enough to pay our bills on time. My going out had simmered down, and we were hosting dinner parties. In fact, a couple of days before my mom went into the hospital; she was supposed to come over for dinner but didn't have the energy or ability to leave her apartment. Shortly thereafter she was hospitalized and later passed on. The blessing was that I had come to the realization that she had done her job. It was time for me to step up to the plate and practice the values and morals she instilled in me and know that even though she was gone, God was still here.

Dilcy Mae Vereen was a great woman, teacher, mother, and friend; she did her job well. She held in there and was able to see me cleaned up and able to stand on my own as a woman, a mother, a wife, and a daughter. Michael and I tried not to let her know all the negatives we had in our marriage, but she was a good ear for both of us and listened to us vent. She was an awesome mother and loved all her children unconditionally. She is gone, but never forgotten. Rest in peace, Mom.

It was also time for me to step up and be a mom to my first son, which I was excited about. Of course, my son was her son, but now was the time for me to make my mom proud. We were still on Carrot Street, but that was supposed to be only our transition house until the one we really wanted was finished. After being on Carrot Street for a few months, I was ready to move into our house on Cedar Street, which was much bigger. I was ready to get the boys settled in and start my classes at college. A few months later I gave birth to my daughter Princess.

After I cleaned up, things seemed great between Michael and me and we began to have a little more romance. He tried to make me happy and even do things that I liked. He took me out to a Jamaican club, we went out to nice restaurants and even a few concerts with big name artists. I just knew I was in love all over again. Michael and I had our ups and downs, but when it was good between us it was really good. Michael was an awesome father, and did his best to provide and protect us. On a couple of occasions he sent me to Jamaica to meet his family for two weeks at a time. We often did things with the kids; they had birthday parties at various places like McDonald's and Chuck E. Cheese. We took videos, tons of pictures and also traveled together as a family. Once, when we visited New York trying to get to Great Adventure in our blue Ford Taurus station wagon, we got there too late. We weren't too disappointed because what ended up being more valuable was our time together as a family. We would host the annual holiday dinner parties for Thanksgiving and Christmas. We gave gifts and cooked big dinners for our entire family, it was awesome, and we all have great memories to share because of it. If you were on the outside looking in you couldn't tell we had any problems, but I did.

My mind still needed to be renewed and I often saw things from only my perspective. Whether I was right or wrong, and clearly a lot of the time I was wrong, I wanted everyone to see things my way, and I wanted everything done my way. I had no understanding of what true and real love was. I needed help, the help that could only come from God.

However, I started feeling like I was alone in my marriage again. I had to have total control at all times, and if things weren't going my way I didn't feel loved. It is not right to have such a controlling personality, but at that time I didn't know that. I thought I was unhappy with Michael because I wanted a man who went to work every day, a man I could have fun with, a man who was proud of me. He wasn't proud of me; at least I didn't feel he was, but I couldn't blame him. In reality, when he disagreed with me or disapproved of something I did, I took it as rejection and retaliated with more bad behavior.

It was a destructive cycle, and our marriage went through a lot, mostly because of my poor choices or addiction, but I still wanted him to believe we could be good again. I began to feel distant because I had to work so hard to help provide for our family, and I began to resent him. Michael did hustle up our necessities. He found a way to get them, so I concentrated on the bills. When I was on drugs, he stayed and was there for the kids, and I constantly felt like I owed him. But I needed more. I wanted stability, and though our lifestyle appeared to be normal and stable, it was not. I wish I knew then that I Corinthians 13:4-7 says, "Love is patient, love is kind. It does not envy, it does not boast, it is not proud. It does not dishonor others, it is not self-seeking, it is not easily angered, and it keeps no record of wrongs. Love does not delight in evil but rejoices with the truth. It always protects, always trusts, always hopes, and always perseveres."

Behind closed doors, we were fighting like we were enemies, hurting each other with words and spiteful behavior. Once or twice it actually got physical, but I learned early on to fight back, so it was rare. Instead of communicating effectively and trying to work through it, I started going out again, as soon as I fully recovered from giving birth. My sister gave birth to her daughter, Empress, two weeks before I delivered Princess. While she was in the hospital pushing, I was beside her, wishing I could give birth. I did, of course; I just had to wait my turn.

After we were healed up, it was back to the clubs for us, and that's the way it continued.

I became so unhappy that I filed papers for a divorce, but I never could go through with it. I put the idea back on the shelf for a while, but our fights were sometimes unbearable. The verbal and emotional abuse was terrible. I don't think he knew that his words and insults beat me down. We both were in a vicious cycle trying to accomplish the same thing—control. He thought that by verbally abusing me, it would shame me into doing right by him, and I thought that my actions for attention would show him how desperately I needed him to do what I wanted. He repeatedly told me he had taken me out of the gutter when I was a nobody on drugs with one pair of shoes to call my own, and that he had made me who I was. My response to that was, "Don't flatter yourself!" We were lost, blind, and immature.

Through each trial I gained a little more strength, and through each tribulation I gained knowledge and wisdom, and through time I gained understanding. So no, it was not totally Michael. He was a great dad, and at some points he was a good husband. I don't know what I expected from him. I know Michael pulled away because of my cheating, and I cheated because he was pulling away, but we could have and should have met each other somewhere in the middle.

We moved again to Green Street to a nicer house, then we decided to move back to Bethlehem. That was exciting for me. After all the years since I stopped using crack cocaine, it was the first time I ever gave thought to going back to Bethlehem to live. We were ready to move forward, though, and leave the past behind us. We went house hunting and found an old house that was being remodeled. It didn't have a bathroom or kitchen. The house had been gutted. I was so excited about moving back to Bethlehem I didn't care what the house looked like. I saw the landlord's vision after he explained the setup of the house and how he was fixing it up. I knew I wanted it, even before it was finished. When we went back home, I was happy and just ready to move in. The kids were excited too. The bus stop was right in front of the house, so they would have to go only a few steps to catch the bus. It seemed perfect.

Despite our differences, Michael and I were making it work for our children. He loved his kids, and it showed. He provided them with clothes and shoes. I paid the bills and did pretty much everything else. Every now and again, he would give me a couple hundred dollars he made from gambling. I was still lonely, though, and I tried to mask it; but eventually I would become enraged again, just wanting a man who could do more than I was doing. With Michael, things were the way they were for so long, I think it was impossible to expect it to be any other way. He was stuck in his ways, I was stuck in mine; and those are ingredients for disaster.

To get my hair done, I had to travel to New York. The first time I went to get my hair done, Michael went with me. When we were happy, we were really happy; and even if things were not going so well, no one knew it because we dealt with things and moved on. We took a bus to Manhattan in New York and then the subway to 125th Street to the Africans to get my hair done. We were like young lovers again, spending quality time with each other. It took them seven hours to do my hair, and Michael stayed with me, then we headed back home.

When the time came for me to get my hair done again, Michael did not feel like being there all day. I asked his uncle to drive me in my car. He drove me the next time as well. A couple of months later, I couldn't get anybody to go and had to go alone. I was scared, but I did it. After I got on the road, I realized that it wasn't as difficult as I originally thought. I found my way back to 125th Street. I found a shop that I could remember how to get to and went there for a long time. Once I got comfortable with the drive to New York on my own, I started taking my sisters. Then I realized if I could make the drive to get my hair done, I could make the drive to hang out but not like back in the day. After that, my sisters and I frequently traveled to New York. I know Michael regretted my figuring out I could make that drive on my own. I no longer needed a chauffeur or escort, and that meant I had nobody to keep tabs on me. Now that I could make that drive on my own, I was able to explore New York. I no longer had the fear of the road.

One day I was up there with my sister Buffy, who wanted to come along for the drive. On the drive back home we were sitting in traffic, and I looked to my right and saw a Jeep Wrangler double-parked near our turn to get back on the parkway to go home. I noticed a guy with brown dread locks, and brown skin and for some odd reason I was stuck on him. I rolled down the window, and the guy and I quickly exchanged words and numbers. As soon as I pulled away, he called me. I told him where I was, and he came to me immediately. I pulled over and got out and got into his vehicle. I felt I could trust him, and we talked a bit more and then I got out. It was a completely innocent conversation we had, and he appeared to be a nice guy; so I programmed his number into my phone. His name was Anthony, though I called him Ant. He was from the Dominican Republic. After I got back into my Camry, my sister and I headed back home. An hour into the drive, he called to check on me, and I told him when I got home I would call him.

I told Ant from the beginning that I was married. I still wore my ring. It didn't seem to matter much. He said he still wanted to know me. Amazingly, it never dawned on me that his being okay with me being married meant he felt free to use me in any kind of way. In other words, if I was sleeping with him, it was okay that he slept with other women too, because I was married and had somebody. I never gave thought to the fact that he might cheat because I thought I was doing the right thing. All I wanted was love, attention, and affection and to feel pretty and I thought that was what I was getting from him. Yet all I was really doing was passing the time for him. Once he found someone he really liked, it would be just a matter of time before he became serious with her and I would be completely out—unless I chose to stay and deal with it. On one occasion I did deal with it.

I used to travel Highway 22 to get to Highway 78 East straight into New York City. It was always exciting. It was a sense of release for me. Michael knew I was leaving and wouldn't say much. I lied to him in the beginning, but after a while he knew and just allowed me to keep going. So I went, believing it was because he was doing his own thing. Besides, when we were home together, we were always arguing. He was happy as long as I was happy, it seemed, and going to New York made me happy. I would make sure I had a full pack of cigarettes for the ride and my music, and I would be on my way to the gas station to fill up. After that I was headed toward the highway. When I would leave, I didn't worry about the kids. I knew Michael had them, and the older ones were big enough to take care of the younger ones when needed. The house was tidy and clean, the kids were in check, and I had no worries. I would leave money for extras and make sure Michael had money in his pocket. I would pack my overnight bag, and I was out of there.

That went on for three years. Then things began to come to a halt. I guess because Ant knew I was still legally married to Michael, he didn't feel like I had the right to snoop, but every time he left I was all over his room, just searching. If you search long and hard enough, you will usually find what you are looking for. My intuition told me Ant was cheating. I know that in such a case sometimes you may be right and sometimes you may be wrong. I also know that you can accuse someone of cheating out of your own guilt. In that case, I was right. I assumed he didn't call it cheating because I had somebody else myself. I was going through his phone and came across a picture of a girl with only a sheet tied around her body sitting on what looked to be his bed. I compared the picture to his little apartment I was sitting in, and sure enough it was his bed she was sitting on, the same bed he had me in. I began to go through the numbers. As I scrolled through his incoming and outgoing calls, I came across a girl he called Mama or some little pet name. I called the number and then hung up. The girl actually called right back. I answered, and she said, "Hi, baby."

I took the phone into the shower, where he was bathing, and asked him about her. Of course, at first he denied it. I threw his phone against the wall out of rage, but I still wasn't satisfied because I knew he was cheating on me. We continued arguing. I was in shock because I had been traveling miles to get to him. I know it was more of a getaway for me, and I was glad I had somewhere to get away. But he was still portraying himself as my man, so I felt he should have carried himself accordingly. Finally, the thing that really set me off was his saying, "She is my girl." Without warning, I punched him right in the face. He tried to shove me back, but he couldn't control me. When I screamed at the top of my lungs, he escaped to the bathroom and sat in there for a while. Later he came out and got the knives, as if I were going to grab for one. I had calmed down some by that point, however. I was still angry and shocked and let off some steam, but I was a lot calmer than before. A bit later he came out of the bathroom, headed for the front door, and left. I saw it as an opportunity to gather everything I had up there, and I left. I had the girl's number memorized, and she and I had some words my whole ride home. In fact, even after I got home, we were still calling one another back and forth.

That was the first time something like that had happened to me. I didn't expect it. I thought I was in love with Ant, and I thought he loved me too, but I was wrong. Meanwhile, Michael was still there. I wanted so badly to stop cheating on him, but I truly didn't know how. I was trying to change, but I still cheated. Indeed, I had become addicted to the attention of other men. Again I had simply exchanged one addiction for another. Ant and I stopped talking for a while. I was hitting the club scene pretty hard, and Michael was doing his own thing once again. I didn't care as long as the kids were okay. That was how we were living for some time and our children didn't even know, and if they did they didn't talk about it to us.

Some months later, out of the blue I got a phone call from Ant. At first I was reluctant to take the call because I had proof he was cheating, and it wasn't just my imagination. However, I had developed some strong feelings for him, so I was happy he called. We talked some and addressed what had taken place some months earlier. I forgave him, and he forgave me, and I was back on Highway78 East that next weekend.

CHAPTER 16

A Real Change

You can't make positive choices for the rest of your life without an environment that makes those choices easy, natural, and enjoyable. ~ Deepak Chopra

Something had begun to happen inside of me. When I would look at Michael, all I wanted to do was cry and stop hurting him. I wanted to change. I wanted to do better, but just because I got off the drugs didn't mean I had the proper help I needed to function in society as a good wife. I was working for an agency that helped mentally challenged and mentally handicapped people. I had started there in 2002 and worked there for five years. I loved it, but something was still missing. I was still trying to get right, but it wasn't all coming together yet. I was still having issues with wanting the attention of other men and still going back and forth, to and from New York. There was still a void in my life. I was in church then but not totally committed. I didn't know it at the time, but I was living a worldly life and enjoying it, despite the dangers, seen and unseen.

Then I began to get the idea in my head of moving. Michael told me about his sister, who was living in Georgia. He told me Georgia was a much nicer place to live and the houses were beautiful. He thought that would be a good move for us, so I decided to go to Georgia with him to visit. We got a sitter, and Michael and I filled the car with gas and got on the road, headed for Georgia. That move was supposed to fix our marriage, make me faithful, and help him get a job. It was supposed to turn our lives around miraculously. I was excited. I looked forward to what was going to be our new life.

We arrived in Georgia thirteen hours later. It happened to be snowing and was cold, but none of that mattered because it was a new start and I was all for it. We reached his sister's apartment, where we were going to be staying while we searched and learned about Georgia a bit and what we were going to need to move to Georgia. Things were going great. We got hooked up with a Realtor and looked at some homes. I was sold. The houses were big and beautiful. They were like dream homes, and I wanted one. After we decided on a home, the next step was doing a contract. I gave the lady my $400 in earnest money. I was moving fast, and Michael didn't try to stop me. It was my money, so he was just going along with the ride. I wanted the house we had picked so badly, I gave false information. I had to have a Georgia address for the past two years, and we produced one. I was just lying and paying as I went along.

I don't care how smart you think you are your lies will be exposed. When they ran my credit report, it came up that I had a Pennsylvania driver's license. Then the truth began to reveal itself. I had already given the loan officer the inspection money of about $400, and I ended up losing all that. To make matters worse, the Realtor told me I needed to give him $200 to fix my credit score. Like an idiot, I listened and sent the money when we got back to Pennsylvania. I actually believed I was going to get away with all the lying. I was so wrong. I had paid out $1000, which I lost when the deal fell through. I ended up with nothing because of my own deceit. I was so wrong to ever think I was going to be able to get away with the deception.

After taking that loss, I had to wait for several months. Then I began to go about things differently. I took my time and was not anxious anymore. I knew what I wanted, but I also knew it was going to be a process. I followed the correct steps and measures and was truthful that time, and everything went smoothly. I didn't have to lie to get my blessing. I was truthful and patient, and when the time was right, we were all packed up and ready to move to Conyers, Georgia. I had set up everything from Pennsylvania. We were going to stay in a rental unit. I had signed the lease via fax, and we were good to go. After we got the house packed up, I got a twenty-seven-foot U-Haul truck. Michael and my boys loaded it, and we attached the car on the back of the truck. Michael had five of the kids in the Durango with him and I had two of my boys with me while I drove the rental truck all the way to Georgia. It was raining when we left, but I was so adamant about leaving, it could have been snowing. I was leaving, and my mind was made up.

At first I got upset with Michael because I thought since he was the man he should drive the big U-Haul. When he flat out refused, I had no choice. With God's favor and good grace, we made it safely to Georgia the following day. It took us twenty-four hours to get there. I was so upset with Michael because he wanted to keep stopping. He was complaining that his feet were hurting, but I would turn to him and say, "Are you serious? It's difficult to get this big truck in and out of those little gas stations." But still I stopped more than I wanted. We rested, and he rested. We ate, and he rested some more. There were bathroom breaks, and then it was full speed ahead. Because of the weight of the truck, we couldn't travel very fast. I was aggravated, but I wouldn't give up. When we finally arrived at our destination, the kids were excited, I was excited, and Michael was excited. It was a new beginning for all of us, or so I thought.

When we arrived the freshly cleaned carpet was still wet. I didn't care because we were there and had the keys. After a couple of hours of hanging out next door at his sister's house, we happily began to unload the U-Haul. Though the house we came to wasn't big enough, we made it work. It was a real time to bond with my children and Michael too. It felt like things were really beginning to come together.

The very next day we checked into enrolling the children in school. All seven of my kids were very well behaved and tried to adjust. After a couple of weeks, though, they hated it and wanted to go back home. My children were riding me so hard about packing up and leaving, I just couldn't take it. We started arguing about who wanted to leave and who wanted to stay. Then, finally, I said, "Look, I am the mama. When you turn eighteen or graduate, whichever comes first, then you can go back." Then I revised it and said, "There are only two ways out of this house: the service or college. Take your pick." There were attitudes in the air, but I didn't care because I was determined to be different, to be a better parent, and to change my ways the best I could, and that was the bottom line.

I was still talking to Ant around that time but not as often because we were miles and lies apart from each other. I knew the move was going to be the cause of our breakup, but I didn't care because I wanted to do better by Michael and be a good wife. Things were going well for a while, and I was talking less to Ant. Then one day I called him, and a girl answered. When I asked to speak to Ant, she asked me why I was calling her man. I was dumbfounded. I said, "Your man? Girl, please, that is my man." We went back and forth with the words and phone calls. She was cussing me, and I was doing my best to keep up, with the exception of the cussing, because I never cussed. I wasn't her match, but my triplet sister, who was visiting at the time, was her match. I told Liana what was going on, and because she gets her point across with the same tone of words, I let my sister beat that girl down with the same words she was throwing at me. Things got quite messy vocally. Ant, of course, denied it for a time but then came out and said she was his girlfriend. I was tired of that and was glad I had made the decision to relocate. Things were going to be different. I was too far away to just get on the road and run to New York. I was forced to let go of that relationship, and I did, slowly but surely.

The kids were all enrolled in school. We got the proper credits transferred for the bigger boys, and I was excited. That was my new life and new beginning. I continued shopping around for a bigger house and found one in Cobb County. It was a nice one too, a five-bedroom house with a split foyer sitting on a half of an acre of land. It was a rental, but by being where we were, I was able to take my time and search for a house we wanted, and I found one. There were nice trees everywhere, the grass was well groomed, and there was a lot of sunlight coming into the house. In the master bedroom was a beautiful master bath with a Jacuzzi tub. It was a big spacious bathroom with a stand-up shower off to the right. I thought it was really worth the long drive, the arguing, and the headaches. It was all paying off. I came up with the deposit and the first month's rent, and we signed the rental agreement/lease and moved in. The whole time I still had in the back of my mind that Michael better act right now. I was not putting up with what I put up with before. He needed to provide financially. I needed a man I could depend on and one who would be a great example to my boys. I just began to look at life differently.

After we were all moved in, I just waited for one of his moments, and sure enough the cussing and the mental and emotional abuse soon kicked in. He told me how he had taken me out of the gutter and got me off drugs, and then he said something I will never forget. He knew my past. I told him everything and kept nothing from him. I felt obligated to be honest, brutally honest. I got past the lying. I just didn't feel or see the need for it anymore. I had told him years before that I was molested at the age of seven. Now Michael looked at me and told me I started having sex at seven, as if to say I wanted that to happen to me. That was it! I had enough. That was the final straw, and I knew from that moment on that his trying to hurt me in such a way meant the end of our twelve-year marriage.

We were just going through the motions, and when the opportunity presented itself, I was going to get out and be done with it for good. Michael made me believe I couldn't survive without him. He beat up my self-esteem and battered me with words. He might not have known it, but hurt me badly, and it did affect me.

As the days went by, more and more things were being revealed to me. I was still going to clubs and hanging out, but now the things I was doing started to become magnified. I found myself being lonely. I asked Michael to leave after the comments he made, so I was left alone with my children, which was fine. But when nighttime came, the loneliness set in. I had not yet realized that all I had to do was call on Jesus. He had been there the whole time. I just didn't realize it. He had kept me from harm and dangers from the streets and drugs. I was ready to receive better understanding of what God wanted and required of me. I had not yet fully submitted to Him, but I wasn't far from it.

I decided to go out to the reggae club. I thought I was cute and everything was in place including the vehicle I drove. I had the appearance of someone with a lot of money so I used it. On that particular night while in the club on my way to the bathroom I saw a guy who appeared to be a "hot boy". He was Jamaican, taller than me and handsome. We were mutually attracted to each other and we then exchanged phone numbers. The next day I called him, which was a Tuesday and we agreed to meet up with each other for a couple of drinks. After I made sure all was well with my children and in the house, I left to meet him. I set out for the road and in doing so all kinds of thoughts began to bombard my mind. I thought about whether or not it was a good idea but that thought quickly subsided. Then I thought about going to meet a complete stranger by myself with no real protection, but that thought also disappeared a short time later. Finally, I arrived at our agreed upon meeting place. He was driving a gold colored BMW, with very dark tinted windows. As I pulled up he gestured for me to follow him away from the location we were at, so I did. We arrived at a sport's bar; to my amazement it was an American bar, different from the reggae bar that we first met at. I was okay with it because we were going to be around other people. We entered the bar and other people followed us in as well. He asked me if I wanted a drink I said yes. Upon observing him as he stepped up to order a drink I saw a taller guy behind him I thought to myself that it was strange, surely he could feel that man behind him invading his personal space by how close he was pressed up on his back. It was very strange. What I thought I was seeing couldn't be happening. Here was a thuggish, sexy man with another guy pressed up against him acting like he couldn't feel a guy behind him. And I could be assuming but I know what I saw. As time went on and we got our drinks we went over to a spot nearby the dance floor and that's where I stayed while he went back and forth for our drinks. The drinks began to set in and I dismissed what I saw earlier at least for the time and began to dance with him. After a few more drinks and more dancing the club closed. He thought the night was still young however by that time it was about 2 o'clock in the morning. He suggests that we go back to his apartment; he explains that he had an apartment that he used to rent with a room-mate; however the electric was off because he said he wasn't sure he was going to keep the apartment so he let them get cut off. Now in hindsight I see that it was all wrong from start to finish. After following him back to his apartment to my amazement the apartment was still furnished as far as I could see and there were candles everywhere. It looked to me like a hide-a-way spot that nobody was supposed to know about.

We began to get familiar since I had just met him and didn't even know his last name, but after a few drinks it didn't matter. He laid me down and we began to become more intimate, I asked him if he had a condom because I knew what was coming next. He pulled out a condom and opened it in front of me and put it on before we started. After a very short time I heard that voice again that prompted me to check for the condom and to my shock and amazement "the condom was gone." I panicked, I shouted "where's the condom that I saw you put on?" He acted like he was so drunk he didn't understand what I was saying. Without a further thought I jumped up and with tunnel vision headed straight for the balcony. I couldn't process everything that was happening. I cried, I assumed, I thought and then I panicked some more. I gathered my thoughts and then gathered my things and without any notice I left, I don't even remember shutting the door.

I had to get back home where I was safe because I had jeopardized my health, my safety and my self-esteem for a short time of careless fun. I had no idea where I was, all I know is that we drove for a while to get there and finally I found a familiar road and headed home. I was so happy when I pulled into my driveway, however so very afraid because I could have just been exposed to something that could cost me my life. I was so ashamed, so afraid, so confused and couldn't believe that after all I had been through and all I had escaped and all that God saved me from that I had actually put myself in such a dangerous position. I decided that night enough was enough. I stopped going out and that was the beginning to the conviction I started to feel by the Holy Spirit. A transition was beginning to take place. For a while it was about my children only, I still couldn't get over the last encounter. I had to heal mentally emotionally and spiritually because I felt so broken after that. As time went by I found myself beginning to feel lonely again and I just wanted to make things right.

In my loneliness, I told Michael he could come back. I actually believed I really did need him. He came back, but things were never the same. He was back and forth from here to there—Pennsylvania, New York, and other states. Eventually, Michael and I divorced and I remarried, looking for the same validation, attention, and love that I had been searching for since I was a child.

Jumping from one relationship to the next is not a solution or cure for loneliness, and it is wrong and hurtful to the other person involved. You first need to work on yourself, allowing God to fill the empty spaces. I knew I needed order, stability, organization and balance. When things were out of order, I just didn't know how I was going to feel from day to day, and this caused a great deal of confusion. However, I discovered that I still needed to be worked on mentally because I was still unstable, but I refused to give up.

I know that no marriage is perfect, and it takes a lot of hard work and effort from both people involved. As much as we would like things to be perfect, sometimes they are not. We don't know what the future holds, but we can only do our best, live in the present, and make good choices instead of focusing on the negative aspects or being overwhelmed by future plans.

It was during my second marriage, when we were dealing with

a very difficult situation, that I finally surrendered all to God. Up until that time, I was "playing church" and I was growing tired. It was exhausting living a double lifestyle. I was still going to nightclubs, singing in the choir, and believing that I was fine.

However, you can't serve two masters and you definitely can't mix the light with darkness. Either you're going to love one and hate the other or vice versa. I lacked a great deal of understanding, but I was not completely comfortable doing what I was doing either. It was time for me to take the next step, I was ready to turn my life around and truly fulfill my purpose. Under the leadership and covering of Chief Apostle Marion E. Johnson and Sr. Bishop A. Ralph Johnson. I learned that I didn't know it all and that I still had some growing to do.

God saved me for such a time as this, and I began to understand and walk in my purpose, no longer wasting my time, but being transformed. God's not through with me yet. Life is a learning experience and a process and I now know that we are not to give up at the first sign of trouble but to hold on and let God be the God of our lives. Today my mind is renewed and my body restored.

I am standing and fighting. I'm still getting to know myself, and learning to love myself before I can expect others to love me. Sometimes all we have to do is hold on and stand on God's words and promises, and He will see us through. I've also learned not to be so hard on myself, to be patient, and to always find peace. I know that God is love and his love endures forever. I have endured a great many trials and tests, hardships and opposition as well as shame and rejection. This was mostly due to my disobedience, which led me down a dark path filled with hopelessness and uncertainty. There is no way I could have made it out of all of that alive, and in my right mind, on my own. God's Grace really is sufficient, and it is the reason why I am still here today.

I have to thank God daily because I encountered such dangerous situations but He kept me through them all. There are times when I just can't believe that I had been spared. But glory to God, He gave me another chance. Any number of my experiences could have been my end, however, God made them my testimonies and now He gets all the glory for my story. I will never be afraid or ashamed to tell my story with the hopes that maybe one person can find the freedom I have, and experience a real change.

CHAPTER 17

Forgiveness and Deliverance: My Path To Recovery

Forgiveness says you are given another chance to make a new beginning. ~ Desmond Tutu

I was bound up for so long by guilt, shame and fear right along with being unforgiving to others and myself. Because of my poor choices I had to learn the hard way, but God did in fact work them out for my good, once I chose to ask for forgiveness and turn away from those things. Today, because Christ first loved me, I know how to love and be loved; however, I had to also learn how to forgive. Yes, at one point I was victimized; however today I no longer see myself as a victim but a victor. Today I am more than a conqueror. I didn't even realize that I was unforgiving; but like drug addiction or addiction of any kind, you have to come to terms with it and admit to yourself that you have a problem. I was imprisoned by holding on to the pain and the guilt. It laid dormant waiting for the opportunity to destroy me. When you are unforgiving it hurts you more than the person you have not forgiven. It can cause bitterness that will take root all through your body like poison. Do not allow this bondage to consume you; it will destroy you and any chance you have at having healthy relationships with others. You must choose to forgive. Do yourself a favor and do an assessment of everyone who has ever harmed you, persecuted and rejected you in any way. Write down each individual whether it is a close friend a relative or a stranger. Whomever it is that you may not have forgiven, along with their offenses. Upon doing so, forgive each and every one of them so you can move on and be set free.

In the Holy Bible Jesus says in Matthew 6:14 "For if you forgive other people when they sin against you, your heavenly Father will also forgive you."

Forgiving others as well as yourself will help to break those chains of guilt, hurt and shame from your past. No longer do you need to hide those secrets; no more do you have to wear those bruises on the inside.

If ever you find yourself having a hard time forgiving, ask God to help you. This is also why it is so important to be in constant communication with God through prayer. You need to have a real relationship with Him. It's about more than just saying, "Thank you, Jesus!" when everything seems to be going good and working out for you. It's about thanking Him at all times through the good and the bad.

It's time to forgive myself for my past and all the people who hurt me and even the ones who offended me and didn't even know it. I carried that around for so long. I pray that all the people I've hurt in my past will also forgive me so that we can all be forgiven by our Heavenly Father God and move forward. It's time to release it and get free. It's time I forgive myself for not being there for my children the way I needed to be during my active addiction to drugs amongst other addictions and careless living. It's time to forgive myself for harboring that guilt on the inside trying to cover it up causing more pain and destruction. It's also time to forgive my dad, I didn't even know I blamed him for all the times I saw my mother struggling to raise us and even for his addiction. I blamed him. I just didn't understand but later finding myself going through exactly what he went through my eyes were opened and I have a lot more understanding now. The disease of addiction is treacherous and wicked, he was sick but thank God he is clean and sober today; happily married with a new family retired and blessed. He had to go through his seasons to get where he is today as well as I did and all I can say is God did it.

The truth of the matter is you cannot live your life worried about things that took place in the past, we all have to grow and go from level to level by faith to faith. Now I am able to tell my story regardless of the secrets, guilt and shame from my past. I am no longer guilty, angry, bitter and bound up; but free through Christ Jesus!

Recovery is a journey. It is not accomplished in one day, it happens daily. Recovery can also be viewed as being a marathon and not a sprint. It requires dedication work and endurance. Sobriety is the first step to recovery you have to submit and commit to being sober and then recovery is possible. It is not an easy road it requires hard work dedication and change, which will spark growth. Your mind will began to change, the people you once hung around in active addiction has to change, and the places you used to frequent you can no longer visit. Everything becomes different, and this is where deliverance comes in.

First it's Sobriety, then Recovery and then Deliverance. These are the steps I went through before obtaining my deliverance. The bible teaches us that faith without works is dead and that it is impossible to please God without it. By submitting my will and seeking another way, I was able to get sober and the footwork began for total recovery. However, in order to do either of these I had to have faith that there is a better way and that there is someone greater than myself working behind the scenes. God kept me, but I also had a part to do and that was to take the first step to get sober and start recovery.

After a time of working at it and not giving up even when I fell down I still kept trying. I was so tired of hurting the people who were the closest to me, and I was killing myself and forcing them to stand by and watch me do it. Addiction is a demon from Hell and the only way to get over it is to allow God the opportunity to step in and deliver you.

You have to remain steadfast and consistent, never giving up, looking toward a brighter future as I did, it was hard work, but it's something that I've committed myself to. Most people think of deliverance as some miraculous awakening, and one day you just don't want to use anymore, one day you wake up and you're cured of all addictive habits and urges. Well you have to go through some phases before you can reach that point as I did. It is just as much work as any other way to recovery, and you have to want it. I've been down so many paths, and I've tried just about everything to fill the hurt, pain, and emptiness that developed from years of disappointment and bad decisions. I've also tried just about every other step and path to recovery, but I've only found one way that worked for me. Complete and total surrender of my will to God. God plays a huge part in my recovery; however, I'm just as much an active participant in my own recovery. That means that I have work to do, both mental and physical. You can't expect to become new in mind, body and spirit with the same old mindset.

A great example of this is weight loss. When a person is obese for reasons such as unhealthy eating habits, or addiction to food and their life is at risk, they have a decision to make. Continue eating the same way and living the same lifestyle, which could lead to an early death, or lose the weight and live a healthier, happier life. There are many options for losing weight. You have medication, surgeries, exercise, diets, therapy, or a combination of any of these. You have a choice to make, and it's not which option you will take; the question is will you commit?

Although your life depends on it, and even though it is hard work, will you choose life? The doctor can remove the fat or make your stomach smaller, but you have to change your mind, and your thinking about food. If you have an unhealthy or abusive relationship with food, and are not ready to completely change your thinking and your lifestyle, then no matter what the doctor does, you will return to what feels good and is familiar to you. You will probably gain all of the weight back again if you don't commit to eating better and regular exercise. It takes discipline and a complete change of lifestyle if you want lifelong results, and it's not always that easy.

God was and is my doctor, but after my consultation with him, I chose to do the work that it took to guarantee a clean sober life. I wanted to be a better person; I wanted to stop causing my family hurt and pain. I wanted my children back in my life, and I wanted to be able to truly say that I can do all things through Christ that strengthens me. I was ready to fight to get my life back.

I wanted to share with you some of my life's journey. There were experiences that I revisited and even I wondered how I made it through all of that and how I am still alive? Did that really happen? How could I have survived? I know beyond a shadow of a doubt that it was God who kept me, even when I didn't care enough to keep myself.

My story is not one for those who want a watered down version of the life of a used-to-be addict. It's for those who are struggling or those who know someone who is struggling with addiction and feelings of worthlessness and low self-esteem, and is willing to try a road to recovery that is less traveled. It is for those who want to know how someone could have gone through all that I did, and survive. It is for someone who needs to know that if God can do this for me, He will do it for you. This is why I am not ashamed of my story; it must be told so that souls will be saved.

I am at a point in my life where I am learning to surrender daily. I am not perfect in fact I am far from it, but it doesn't stop me from trying. Every day I am growing and changing into the woman that God has planned for me to be. We never stop growing and the most important thing is that we remain teachable. I have definitely changed and I love it.

CHAPTER 18

Encouragement

No weapons formed against you shall prosper, and every tongue which rises against you in judgment You shall condemn. This is the heritage of the servants of the Lord, and their righteousness is from Me," Says the Lord. ~ Isaiah 54:17

The domestic violence was a weapon; the emotional and mental abuse were weapons; poverty was a weapon; the drugs and sexual addictions were weapons; the attention seeking became a weapon as well as low self-esteem. They were all weapons, however God didn't allow any of them to prevail or prosper against me because I am still here today healthy, alive and in my right mind, raising my children to love and honor God.

I have had many trials and tribulations in my life, and God has seen me through each and every one of them. If it had not been for my mother's prayers keeping me lifted before God while I was out there on the streets, I don't know where I would be. I can certainly testify to the fact that it is by the grace of God that I am here today.

Things have changed so much for me. I am no longer the downtrodden little girl with low self-esteem. I am living in my dream home. I have a degree in Criminal Justice Administration. Today, I have a full governor's pardon, which I obtained a year after coming to Georgia. I am experienced in working with mentally and physically handicapped individuals. I worked with them for five years prior to coming to Georgia. Two years after moving to Georgia, I got my CNA (certified nursing assistant) license. It was tough earning the license, but I have a strong desire to help people, so this field fits my personality. I now have experience in hospice care, working with people who are dying, as well as elderly men and women in need of private home care and health care services. It is also my desire to teach young adults as well as women and men who may feel that they are too bad to be saved. The reason for our relocation was to fix and external problem when all along the problem was internal. I had to renew my mind. I had to change my mindset which is an ongoing process however, as long as you don't give up things will always get better in spite of the trials and tests that may come. There are many people that can learn from my mistakes, especially our youth.

After experiencing life as a nurse's aide, I became a business owner, purchasing precious metals, (gold, silver and platinum). I now work in Ministry helping others, writing, and furthering my education in Psychology: Substance abuse and Life Coaching. It is my passion and mandate to help people, mostly because I have been there and can see many of the issues from the inside out.

My oldest son Laquan graduated from high school and is now working for a prestigious company. He is paving his own way and making responsible and mature decisions. He has grown into a very bright and intelligent young man of whom I am very proud.

Next in line is Devon. He is now in his senior year of college, studying Biology and Spanish. He is living in his very first apartment, on his own. He is set to graduate with two degrees. I am really proud of Devon because when he was in 4th grade, the teachers informed me that my son had a learning disability and needed special education classes. Devon was determined to prove them wrong and he did; not only did my son take honors courses while attending High school, he also graduated with honors with a 3.58 grade point average. God is so good to me.

My third son, Marsell, completed his senior year in high school as a varsity football player. He enlisted in the United States Navy immediately after high school and is now serving our country. Marsell is very goal oriented and determined and in so many ways helped me even when he didn't understand. God used him to help me see myself and for that I am thankful.

My fourth son, Baby Boy, like me, he had to find his way. Thankfully, he is back on track and has also graduated high school. He may have taken a turn due to rebellious behavior however, let's face it so did I, but thank God he learned a lot sooner than I did. He didn't have to endure the things that I had to go through. I'm so thankful for all the help I did have until I was able to do it for myself.

My fifth son Daquan, graduated high school, and has grown to be a very responsible, hardworking, loving young man. Not only does he work, he cooks, cleans, sews, and really loves his mama. This means so much to me when I know I was such a disappointment to the times, yet they have forgiven me and show me so much love.

My five oldest sons have all graduated and finished high school. Only my son Kenny who is now in the 9th grade and my daughter are left to finish their primary education. Kenny, my sixth son, is in high school and on the right path. He is filled with so much love. I am very proud of how well he is doing in school and just in general, my cuddly bear. And last but not least is Princess. She is my only girl, the youngest child, and full of personality; she is truly a little princess. She is what I have always wanted in a daughter. She is my best friend and even sometimes my greatest critic.

I have to thank God for my children. I wasn't always the best mother, but they never judged me; they stood by my side and show me daily unconditional love, in spite of my past. There were so many great moments that we shared back then but I felt what I did share in this book needed to be exposed to help someone else that might be struggling with past shame, hurt, guilt and disappointment.

I told my son Marsell on a Skype call one day that some of the content in this book was very shameful, embarrassing and even hurtful to others and myself. He said to me, "Mom we are moving forward, and that was your past. They were obstacles that you overcame to get you where you are today." It meant so much to me for him to understand this. Instead of rejecting me and blaming me as his mother he accepts me and respects me no matter what. We are moving forward! I am so very proud of all seven of my children.

Truly, today I am a better woman, wife, mother, teacher, Christian and now Evangelist. I owe God so much because without Him in my life, there would be no me. I am nothing without Christ Jesus. I have gained more strength, growth, knowledge and wisdom, more values and morals, and respect for others and myself. I have also learned how to love myself so that I can love others. I respond to being respected instead of being rejected. God has turned my entire life around. Today I am not the woman I used to be. Today I am a child of the Most High God, and I rejoice in that. Today it doesn't matter who wants to reject me because I know my Father in heaven accepts me. Today I am loved, wanted, and appreciated. Today I am more than a conqueror. Today I am the head and not the tail. Today I am above and not beneath.

Today my tests are my testimonies. Today I am who God says I am, His child.

In telling my story, my hope is to empower young adults, men and women all over the world who fall victim to judgment, rejection, ridicule, embarrassment, and or shame. I am here to tell you that you do not have to see yourself as a victim. In fact, you can start seeing yourself as a victor. After all, God made us to be more than conquerors. However, in order to conquer something, you have to go through something. I have been through many storms. I have been rejected, and made to feel unwanted and at one time forced to believe I was worthless and wasn't going to make it. But guess what! I am a living witness to testify today that those were all lies. I had to endure the fire and affliction to get to my rightful place. I am by no means perfect and won't be until I get to heaven, but I am sure my ending will be better than my beginning and my best is yet to come.

I often hear people say they wish they could go back to when they were younger. Not me, I don't care to repeat any of that, but neither do I regret it, because no matter how you slice it I had to go through all that I have been through in order to learn from it, grow from it, and live because of it. I have learned to turn a negative into a positive. However, I never would have made it through if it had not been for God's unmerited and unprecedented favor. I am chosen as God's vessel to tell you there is nothing impossible with God. All you have to do is believe, and you will receive exactly what God has for you. I can't say you won't have to go through some difficult things to get there, but I will say that you will make it, I did.

When I was a little girl, I was loved very much by my family. However, when I left the house, I was picked on at school and made to believe I was different from other kids—too big, too fat, or too poor. These were all lies, but I made it. When I was fourteen years old, I made some careless choices that could have cost me my life, but I made it. I got into an abusive relationship that could have been my end emotionally, physically, mentally, and spiritually, but I made it. I entered the drug scene and lost all control. People began to talk about me, treat me like I was nothing, and say I wasn't going to make it. They counted me out, but I made it because God counted me in. I went from club to club, drank while driving, slept with different men, took risks I normally wouldn't have done had I been in a sober state of mind, and just ran free, but I made it. I would get on the long highway, driving back and forth to and from New York, seeking companionship when I was already married. I was running from loneliness when all the while I was simply trying to run from myself. But I made it.

This is a book about obstacles and opposition, trials and triumphs. Some may be tempted to judge me because of my past but keep in mind it is my past. Everyone has a past. I am on display for Christ and I don't want to hide anything, this is how I have gained my deliverance, by being honest with others and now myself. I have a whole new sense of freedom and endless hope. God did this for me. He saved me from a life of no hope and brought me into a life with great promise. I have no regrets. I have learned to accept my faults and to forgive others as well as myself. Today I live on purpose and today I have purpose.

So when you see me praising, and worshiping God, it is not for fame, fashion, or style, it is because He loved me and taught me how to love Him. I have real happiness and joy and now I know how to love myself. I am thankful for all I have been through because it has made me who I am. Some people might even think that all my shouting, jumping, and dancing is not necessary, but I am here to tell you it is necessary. It is because of God's grace and His mercy that I am alive and able to shout, sing, praise, and dance. Today I am truly free and no longer Lost In The Valley!

"It doesn't matter where you came from; what matters is where God is taking you!" - Evangelist Ivana Vereen

From The Author

Thank you for reading this book. I hope it has been a blessing to you. Maybe it has opened your eyes to what anguish and turmoil a loved one has gone through, or maybe you have struggled or are struggling with addiction. If you are looking for a way out of a lifestyle that will lead to a certain death, and have tried traditional recovery methods, I invite you to try Jesus. You too can surrender all to him. If you are ready to accept Jesus into your life and begin a mind renewing, life changing process say this prayer:

"Lord Jesus, I thank you for sparing my life. I thank you for keeping and protecting me even when I made bad choices. I've suffered a lot, and been through so much pain throughout my life, and I'm tired. I'm tired of living this way. I do not have the strength or power to do this alone, I need your help. I am a sinner. I believe that Jesus died for my sins. God, please forgive me of my sins, and help me to also forgive myself. Remove the people and things out of my life that lead me to temptation. Help me to be strong and resist even when it seems harmless. Send new people and things in my new life that will foster a positive healthy lifestyle. I love you and I am beginning to love myself. Help me to now shine my light, do good to others, and make a difference in this world. In Jesus' name I pray, Amen."

If you said this prayer or are considering this path to recovery, I would love to hear from you. If this book has impacted your life in a positive way, I would love to hear your testimony. To connect with me, or for more information, additional resources, bulk sales, or booking Ivana to speak at your next event, visit www.IvanaVereen.com

Resources

Below you will find some helpful resources. You can also find more resources on my website www.IvanaVereen.com.

Substance Abuse and Mental Health Services Administration
SAMHSA.gov
1 877 726 4727
1 800 487 4889 (TDD)
M-F 8:30 AM to 5:00 PM
findtreatment.samhsa.gov
SAMHSA National Helpline
1 800 662 HELP (800 662 4357)
TTY: 800 487 4889

Teen Drug Abuse
http://teens.drugabuse.gov/

New Directions Treatment Services
2442 Brodhead Road
Bethlehem, PA 18020-8910
Phone: 610-758-8011

Domestic Violence: (national and international)
The National Domestic Violence Hotline 24/7
Confidential Support
www.thehotline.org
1 800 799 SAFE (1 800 799 7233)
TTY 1 800 787 3224

Child Abuse National Abuse Hotline
http://www.childhelp.org/hotline/
The Child Help National Child Abuse Hotline
1 800-4-A-CHILD (1 800 422 4453)
Is dedicated to the prevention of child abuse.

National Child Sexual Abuse Helpline - Darkness to Light
www.d2I.org
1 866-For-LIGHT (1 866 367 5444)

SAMHSA Centers and Offices
Center for Behavioral Health Statistics and Quality
240 276 1250
Center for Mental Health Services
240 276 1310

Center for Substance Abuse Prevention
240 276 2420

Center for Substance Abuse Treatment
240 276 1660

Teen Pregnancy:
National Dating Abuse Helpline/ Teen Chat line
www.loveisrespect.org
1 866 331 9474

National Runaway Safeline 24/7
www.1800runaway.org
1 800-Runaway (1 800 786 2929)

Breast Cancer Information
breastcancer.org
Cancer Treatment Centers of America 24/7
1 888 847 7403
www.cancercenter,com
1 888 940 6255

HIV/AIDS:
CDC National AIDS Hotline 24/7
1 800-CDC-INFO (1 800 232 4636)
TTY 1 888 232 6348
English and Spanish
www.cdc.gov/hiv/

AIDS Activities Office of Lehigh Valley Hospital
17th & Chew Streets
Allentown, PA 18102
Phone: 610 969 2400

HIV/AIDS Hotlines and other Resources-Project Inform
www.projectinform.org/hotlines/

Atlanta STD Testing- Same Day No Appointments Needed
100% confidential
www.stdcheck.com/Atlanta
1 800 456 2323
Suicide Prevention:
Suicide Prevention Lifeline
1 800 273 TALK (1 800 273 8255)

National Suicide Prevention Lifeline 24/7
1 800 273 8255
English and Spanish
www.suicidepreventionlifeline.org

Disaster Distress Helpline
 1 800 985 5990
TTY 1 800 846 8517

Homelessness:
City Union Mission
Your City. Your Mission
Men, Women and Families
816 474 4599
www.cityunionmission.org/services/hotline-for-the-homeless

Veterans Crisis Line
www.veteranscrisisline.net/
1 800 273 8255 press 1

Stop Bullying
http://www.stopbullying.gov/

The Bully Project
http://www.thebullyproject.com/

To Amanda,

It is wonderful to finally meet you. I look forward to working with you!

Best wishes to you!

God bless you!

with love

Van

May 2015